CHILDREN OF GOD

IT'S TIME FOR JUBILEE

BY

PROPHET CYRIL R. HOWELL, SR.

FOREWORD BY SALLY GLENN

EXPAND KNOWLEDGE PUBLICATIONS
WWW.EXPANDKNOWLEDGE.NET

Children of God It's Time For Jubilee
By Prophet Cyril R. Howell, Sr.

Copyright © 2007 Cyril R. Howell, Sr.

Cyril R. Howll
1508 Bowmore Place
McLeansville, NC 27301

ISBN 978-0-6151-6273-7

Acknowledgements

First of all, I would like to thank the Lord Jesus Christ for being my strength and the Holy Spirit for being my source of revelation and Father God for finally releasing me to put in print some of the rich treasure He has shared with me concerning the Word of Life, the Holy Bible.

To my parents, the late Paul and Betty Howell, my brothers and sisters, who always have a pleasant place in my memories, and to my many maternal and paternal uncles and aunts.

To my wonderful grandmother, Gertrude, who went home to be with the Lord while I was writing this book.

To my loving, and enduring wife, Jacque, who has been through many birth pangs with me. Without your inspiration and moral support, and assistance I could never have written this book.

To my father-in-law and mother-in-law, James and Jennie Mae Scott — whose love and wisdom have continued to support me after the loss of my parents.

To my children; James, Cyril, Jr., Precious, and Princess who are the source of many of my life's lessons, and the encouragement to write to their generation as well as my own.

To all of the dear saints and friends of Ambassadors Of Life In Christ Church of Greensboro, North Carolina.

To my Spiritual parents, Apostle Steve & Olivia Foreman and the Abundant Life Church of Christ family, Men of Destiny, CAN Conference Leaders, Fifth Sunday Fellowship pastors and all my colleagues in the gospel whom I do not have space to mention each of you. I love you all dearly in the Lord.

Table of Contents

FOREWORD

"Children of God , it is time for Jubilee!" This is the resounding proclamation of Prophet Cyril Howell in this remarkably insightful book. He has truly grasped the heart of God and His great desire to liberate us from captivity and fill us with the fullness of joy.

He presents scriptural feasts as parallels to our progressive walk of spiritual preparation. This leads to a magnificent outcome — the perfection of the church with a testimony of grace. Yes, the Jubilee trumpet is sounding. It should awaken us of the purposes of God in our lives and alert us to be equipped and ready for a mission.

A series of trumpet calls are sounded, as Jesus calls us to a higher place in Him. "What is the trumpet saying? What time is it for the church? What gifts do we need to cherish to let God arise in our lives?" These are questions Prophet Howell addresses.

One trumpet calls us to prayer, beseeching our hearts to bow when our knees are bent. Another arouses us to praise which does not stop with our lips but continues in our lives. The trumpet call of worship resounds to express His glory, unveil its splendor, and reveal its beauty. It is for the heart to be set free.

The call to unity is to be in unity with Christ and each other. It is a call to holiness which heralds us to gather as one family to represent Christ Jesus upon the earth, The trumpet of Jubilee is resounding the voice of liberty to us all. This will bring freedom from the oppressions of life. God is blowing the trumpet of blessing as well, as He speaks His purpose to the church — to declare His faithfulness.

Prophet Howell reveals eight wonderful blessings which can be claimed by every believer. It is truly his desire and the scope of this book to present the concept of Jubilee as a promise to be possessed and enjoyed forever.

Sally Glenn, Christian Author and Prophetess

Preface

As we come toward the turn of this century to close the second century and began the third, we will stand on the threshold of change in our world and in the church. How you will be affected by those changes largely depends on where you stand in relationship to Jesus. For most of us, this time of transference from one century to the other is a rarity we will never experience again, and for others, one that they may make their personal transference from this life to eternity.

This era we live in is full of speculations about our future. It seems no one is certain about anything anymore. Look around you and it becomes so obvious. Let me rewind just a moment to the time span I started these pages. Globally, we are preparing for an economic fallout as Y2K approaches. Here in America, we can simply look at our nation and see the chaotic confusion that is consuming our world. At the very moment I am writing this passage, our nation is struggling about whether or not we will keep our president. Our Congress is dealing, not with moral issues, but an obvious political battle of minds on Capitol Hill splitting right down party lines. As Christians, we ought to know that division is always initiated by Satan, himself, and the devil is an undercurrent in every negative situation.

The church is filled with alternatives and modifications of God's Word, sometimes swaying dangerously toward complete apostasy in our word, worship, walk, and work we do for God. We have stretched the moral boundaries of our beliefs so far that there is a loss of the kind of tension that brings true cohesiveness to Christian living among the people of God.

In our society, we simply live our lives with our different masks and surround ourselves with our defense mechanisms, our security blankets, and our clique of protective supporters of our good or evil. We, as children of God, many times become like the child next door who used to be a playmate, but for some reason no longer wants to come out and play anymore. We have become great imitators, but not great demonstrators of the truth of God's Word. We've talked about many things in our generation, but how much have we really owned up to?

When I look at the state we are in, I realize that there is something more, and I want the Lord to help me and you to experience the "more". If you've been praying for the Lord Jesus to send a real revival and heal our land; if you're in search for a more meaningful existence; if you desire to break the barriers of your own soul, and truly tap into "Spiritual Life in Christ," then your need not only to open up the pages of this book, but the pages of your heart, because God is not through writing His story in my life and your life yet. The best is yet to come!

Children of God, it is time for Jubilee!!!

Prophet Cyril R. Howell, Sr.

Note: This book was written before the September 11th attack on the World Trade Center. It has been preserved in its original format and is still relative for our times in which we live.

INTRODUCTION

The sun shined brightly through an opening between the curtain stirring me from a restless night of tossing and turning in my sleep. My family has already risen, and I can hear the sound of footsteps from room to room. *"They must already be doing their chores."* I think to myself. That's usually the routine since everyone is so busy working and going to school during the week.

I gaze at the clock beside my bed. *"What time is it?"* It is 10:15 a.m. on a Saturday morning. I've slept at least eight hours, but my body seems exhausted. Still I rise and move quickly to take my morning shower. In the shower, I proceed to give thanks and praise for seeing another blessed day in the Lord. *"I've got a busy day."*, I ponder as the waters flow over me. " I have to be at the YMCA soccer field by 11:45 a.m. to coach my team. Then I have to pick up the children for choir rehearsal which starts at 1:00 p.m. Then I have to meet with a friend at another pastor's church concerning this new health care product business at 4:00 p.m. We also have a special Jubilee youth night service at 7:00 p.m. It's a time for the young people to come together at Ambassadors of Life in Christ Church to celebrate their relationship with Jesus Christ.

"Lord Jesus, give me the strength to make it through this day, and please give me a good night's sleep afterward."

Then I look back at what I just asked the Lord to do, and I wonder if indeed I understand that my *time* to do the things I believe are important is very limited, and I'm giving to God the least part of my *time* called *"spare time"*. In fact after I've given my *time* to my job and the school system (whether it be as a teacher or parent), I don't have much *time* left.

"I'll be glad when I have more time doing the things I believe are most important." I thought dreamingly.

Though I have taken a real excerpt from my own life to open this book, I hope that you realize that there are thousands upon thousands of people just like me. *Time* is a precious element of life, and the way we utilize our *time* determines our success and our failure. And though there are many that we call "full- time pastors", there are also many pastors like me, who have full-time jobs, and are still *full-time* pastors. Their work of ministry is also never done. Some pioneering works do not have the privilege of being full time. The call is greater than the *time* given. So whether *time* is accessible to you or not, vision is what sparks our interest in *time*, because, let's face it, we don't live in eternity. It is not how much *time* you have; it is what you do with the *time* you do have!

Now I have come to realize as a Christian that *time* is often a luxury we do not have, and we cannot afford to waste *time* in a generation that truly needs to understand the message of Jesus Christ. How to manage our *time* and still give God His *time* can often be a challenge to each of us. The only true solution is for God to reveal to us *His time*, so that we are in synchronization with Him in His plan. Only God can truly redeem time and bring our purpose to pass *on time*!

Time is equally important in the world we are living. The year 2000 (referred to as Y2K) presented a most evident problem we encountered with time as the economic world raced against time to fix the often mysterious and, to some, overly exaggerated computer glitch we had in converting the numeric sequence to correspond to the turn of the century. Recently in March 2007, we moved the daylight savings time to help save even more energy presumably.

This natural struggle in the time factor is also critical in the spiritual aspect of the church world, while many attempt to predict the coming of the Lord. This attempt is not only in a general sense, but sometimes even to the exact date in time.

While I am not going to deal with eschatological matters, I will prophetically say that I am in agreement that we are living "in the last of the last of days." *Time is winding up!*

In this book, my concern is that we are so controlled by the circumstances in which we live, so much so that we are literally *"enslaved"* by this thing called time, instead of having the ability to truly operate in the realm of eternity with Jesus. We are called to live in Heavenly places, that is, above the dictates of this world. We need to hear what the Father is ushering us to experience in the Holy Spirit. Our goals, dreams, and aspirations should not be orchestrated by a clock on the wall, but rather by the heartbeat of God's great desire in our lives.

The significance of this lies in the children of God understanding that right now God's will is to bring the church into *a time on His prophetic clock called Jubilee.* However, the great obstacle lies in the preparation of God's people to fulfill this promise in a unified, and undefiled way without the oppressive, controlling, often domineering attitudes of those who may hinder such a plan from ever unfolding in the lives of the children of God. Jesus told the church to "occupy until I come!" In other words, we should not be sitting down and waiting, but we should be working in preparation for His coming! But what will it take for us to be ready *for such a time as this*? How far are we off on *God's prophetic time clock* in preparing us for the days that lie ahead for the church of Jesus Christ? How long can the sinner continue to live in sin while running the risk of running *out of time*? How long can you pause in your purpose, or delay your call without forfeiting *the value of time*?

This book is written to spiritually awaken, and then inspire you prophetically in the things the Lord will reveal to you in these pages. If you have ever felt that your time of God's blessings and purpose will never come, this book is written especially for you. I pray you will be enlightened by its pages, that the life-giving force of the Word of God will lift you to new heights in God's will for your life.

Time can become a servant and a friend to you. I believe that God is getting ready to turn things around for you and for me and release us from our greatest and most present enemy with a sure victory. Come and explore with me how *God's timing* has everything to do with Jubilee. You will be able to discover Jubilee and its significance to this church age, and to all believers in Jesus Christ, our Lord.

Children of God, it's time for Jubilee!!!

CHAPTER 1

BLOW THE TRUMPET!!!

(JOEL 2)

Hustled beneath the billowing clouds, the people of Judah have gathered on Mount Zion which once was toppled with the foliage of acacia trees. Now the branches sway in their nakedness while the fragmented brown leaves mix briskly with the ground. The fresh aroma of the flowers can no longer be smelled, nor alternating colors of violet, red, and white seen . The air is still filled with the gallant and glorious resonance of the trumpet piercing the morning breeze with each breath of the herald. The people of Judah await with their elders for the orator's proclamation to speak in a sovereign way concerning coming events. The trumpet stops.

The prophet Joel emerges upon the scene wrapped in a dusty green mantle, carrying a scroll pitted beneath his right arm. His stride toward the front of the crowd brings a descending silence to his audience. As he unfolds the scroll, he can still recall the sound of the recent devastation, the invasion of the locusts. He looks toward the elders who nod an affirmative gesture that it is now time for him to speak. His voice rings with an urgency that is carried with the wind to the ears of God's people:

We start in Joel, Chapter 2, verse 1.

"Blow the trumpet in Zion and sound an alarm in My holy mountain…", he declares.

"…for the day of the Lord is coming and it is at hand.", Joel continued as he raised his hands and resonated his words into the cool breeze.

The people were already greatly alarmed. However Joel wasn't so sure that he had their attention. They knew the grave conditions around them but what would be their response? Joel gazed intensely upon the faces of the people. Would they truly understand why God allowed all their crops to be destroyed before they could gather their bounty in their barns. The locusts had taken everything. How could God let this happen? How could the God of the covenant leave them without the provisions they needed to survive?

Joel wrapped his green mantle tighter around his chest and stood firmly.

'The Lord gives voice before His army and His camp is very great; for strong is the One who executes His word. For the day of the Lord is great and very terrible; who can endure it?

' "Now, therefore," says the Lord, "turn to Me with all your heart, with fasting, with weeping, and with mourning." So rend your heart, and not your garments; return to the Lord your God, for He is gracious and merciful…….

'Blow the trumpet in Zion, consecrate a fast, call a sacred assembly; gather the people sanctify the congregation, assemble the elders.'

*'**Gather the children and nursing babes**; let the bridegroom go out from his chambers and bride from her dressing room.'*

This is one of my favorite scriptures in the whole bible! This excerpt of scripture from Joel Chapter 2, called the day of the Lord, highlights an event like none other in human history. I can imagine that day! The sound of the trumpet caused God's people to be ushered into *a specific place at a specific time*. The gathering is of such great importance that even those still making preparation on their wedding day are invoked, both the bridegroom and the bride to immediately stop what they are doing to come to the mountain!

We realize that to God, timing is everything! God created time for man's existence. God created the sun, moon, and stars. He created day and night. These are very things that control time. Time was included in the garden of Eden before the fall, so time is really not a curse. Contrary to most of our thinking, it is a great blessing to have time. We need time to work; time to think; time to heal; time to laugh and cry.

Genesis 8:22 says, "While the earth remains, seedtime and harvest, cold and heat, winter and summer, and day and night shall not cease."

Ecclesiastes 3: 1 states, "To everything there is a season, a time for every purpose under heaven."

Time is important! Adam had a time he met with God in the cool of the day. Even Satan had a time he could sit down with the host of heaven and give an account of his deeds, according to Job chapter 1. Jesus, Himself, came in the fullness of time to redeem man. So now we see the people of Judah coming forth to the mountain, because there time is now at hand!

What caused this great gathering of God's people? We can see both historic as well as futuristic events in what this prophet named Joel says. First let's look at the historic event. What happened before the trumpet sounded? Joel and the people had witnessed a plague of locusts that devoured the land of its vegetation and left the territory stripped of it's fruitfulness.

For those of you who have never experienced locusts, this type of plague may seem quite foreign to you. Even if you are familiar with a plague of locusts, it may not have been to this extent. Recently I visited my parents in the Lord, Pastor Steve and Lady Olivia Foreman in Richmond, Virginia. They have built a new home outside the city where you have to go see them on purpose, because it is so far in the woods, no one would drop in accidentally. (Of course, they still have a lot of visitors even on purpose!). It was locust season. When outside, all one could hear was locusts. It was the locusts' mating season! Just the sound alone is enough to get your attention! (That's what God wants to do --- get your attention!) This is only a small example of the annoyance locusts can cause.

Historically, locusts have been known to cause extensive damage to crops until they cause great famines. Their estimated damage to crops has been millions of dollars even in the United States. No continent is actually free from the locust plague unless it is extremely cold. In modern times we have found ways to fight locusts through agricultural knowledge, but in underdeveloped countries they still remain a threat.

Joel is declaring the significance of God sending these locusts, "His exceeding great army!" Joel knew that the spiritual state of Judah was as destroyed, decayed, and ruined as the land the locusts had consumed, and he is used of God to sound the alarm to Judah, just as the swarming locust does in a negative sense. In beginning this subject, I boldly declare that many of our churches are so self- centered that only a major devastation will bring them together. That's what it took for Judah to assemble themselves before the Lord! And furthermore, I am not sure how major that devastation will have to be.

Joel contends that the locusts point to a greater truth. This army refers to people. *"A people come, great and strong, the like of whom has never been; nor will there ever be any such after them, even for many successive generations"* (Joel 2:2-b).   First it points to the natural invasion of Judah by a powerful army, possibly the Phoenician or Philistine army who arose in the ninth century. However, as we continue we will see that there is a much greater spiritual significance for us today, which will be discussed later.

Now let's look at the futuristic events in *time,* or more specifically, the prophetic insight of what Joel is saying. Joel declares it to be "a solemn assembly!" This is a "sacred" time, a "holy" moment. The Lord Jesus will return soon and the results of His coming would be both "terrible" and "great". While the scripture seems to be a paradox, it is simply reflecting the condition in which man himself will be when Jesus returns. There are no greater paradoxes than good and evil, the devil and angels, or heaven and hell. The final plan of life will present only two sides for us! There are no middle grounds, no intermediate lines! Likewise during our time, the world is filled with sorrow and destruction, while the family of God, filled with jubilant praise and the awesome glory of God, prepares to enter into it's finest hour!!! Yes in fact, even while in the midst of writing this book, our world is in a time of uncertainty. As time unwinds, these are some events that have occurred.

The year is 1998. The times are filled with erupting politics from our president's proposed impeachment proceedings (President Bill Clinton) to the resignation of Newt Gingrich as the Speaker of the House, and the U.N. air strikes on Iraq led by American troops on December 16th 1998. Our economy, though improving in some ways, has taken several dives this year at the New York Stock Exchange. Global economics have also been affected by Japan's unstable market and recent troubles in Brazilian stock markets.

On September 11, 2001, two hijacked aircrafts flown by terrorists crashed into the twin towers of the World Trade Center buildings in New York.

In 2005, Florida, Louisiana, and Alabama are hit by hurricane Katrina. The city of New Orleans is flooded, partly because of floodwater and the levees breaking that are holding back the waters.

As time has advanced to the year 2006, we are presently living in a post September 11th era. Things are different now, whether we like it or not. We are at war in Iraq until further notice, even though Saddam Hussein is already executed by hanging. We are still searching for Osama Bin Ladin in Afghanistan. We wonder how our presence in the Middle East jeopardizes international security. Israel's tensions mount with the Arabs.

March 23 2007, Iran flexes its nuclear muscles and challenges Britain's presence in their waters by capturing 16 British sailors from a ship. They are later freed on April 5, 2007.

Our churches are said to be, "more sensitive to the Holy Spirit", but in reality less sensitive to one another. Our views of the church are being decentralized by the acceptance of gay marriages and gay clergy. The divorce rate is soaring, racism is still prevalent, abortions are on the rise, and our reaction to these are remarkably as atrocious as the issues and wickedness itself.

Truly we ought to be saying, "What must we do to be saved?" If there has ever been a time we must hear straight from Heaven and be the people God desires us to be in Christ, it is now. Let's look again at our scripture from Joel 2:2-b:

"A people come, great and strong, the like of whom has never been; nor will there ever be any such after them, even for many successive generations"

I contend to you that the children of God are that people. We are that chosen generation! We are living in the dispensation of time called the "church age". We live in an extended time period for mankind called "grace". We must be on a mission to save as many souls as we can while we still have time left.

We are under the Lordship of Jesus Christ, who is our commander and chief. There will never be another people so united in worship to Jesus. The glory of God upon these people is compared to a "flaming fire"! Each person stays in rank and file as they march to the voice of the Lord. There is complete unison to a single command!

How amazing that is!

The Day Of The Lord requires great preparation for the church because of Jesus Christ's soon return. It is very disheartening to see that many of us lack preparation for the most important things in life. As we view the words of the second Chapter of Joel, we can see the destiny Jesus wants to bring the church. Joel chapter 2:28-32 concludes with the dynamics of the outpouring of the Holy Spirit being extended, not only to the man and woman of God, but specifically to the children of God. It depicts a family whose last call is to gather the children for a most important message. Even in the natural, children are an important part of God's plan. Jesus said, "Let the little children come to Me, and do not forbid them, for of such is the Kingdom of God!" (Matthew 19:14).

The Father's desire is to reap a harvest of souls and adopt us into the family of God. Truly He has a purpose for His children. What does it mean to be a child of God in this diverse, prosperous, yet troubled generation? There is an inheritance awaiting the children of God even in troubled times! That is why this book is being written under the guidance of the Holy Spirit! That is why the time is both terrible and great! This same passage of scripture quickly turns to the bride and bridegroom getting ready for a unique event. This book should fill you with such an excitement in what is coming for the saints of God. As we explore the Word of God as our road map, we can learn how to reach our destiny as God's children.

Get ready children of God! It's time for Jubilee!!!

CHAPTER 2

LORD, PREPARE ME!

(LEVITICUS 23:1-44; 25:1-55)

How do we become such a glorious people in Christ as mentioned in Joel chapter two? We must be prepared! We don't want to be found unprepared like the children of Judah with the coming of the locusts. How should we approach this spiritual journey as God's children?

"We have set our destiny to be that incomparable, progressive, motivated, diligent, uncompromising, supportive, unstoppable, organized, strategic people who are coming with great strength in the name of Jesus Christ! Our mission is now to establish a way of preparing our hearts to be this beautiful, glorified church ultimately called the bride of Christ."

How do we grow up as a young child in the eyes of our Father to a mature bride, glistening in the beautiful light and reflecting the image of our husband, Jesus Christ. I look at my daughters, Precious and Princess, and I can imagine the beautiful brides they will become one day, as they keep their eyes on Jesus. (My daughter Precious has now become exactly that; a beautiful bride). The time of preparation for that glorious day will be worth every moment spent when preparing for a worthy groom. Jesus is our worthy groom, the King of kings and Lord of lords. I look forward to the day I will witness their weddings to husbands who will cherish them as brides, as much as I have as a father. The Son, Jesus Christ, cherishes the church as much as the Father cherishes us as His dear children.

Certainly, the Holy Scriptures teach us about spiritual preparation in a number of ways. Our approach will mainly deal with the progression of spiritual preparation seen in Scripture through the feasts mentioned in Leviticus. If we are going to mature as children of God, the sincere milk of these words from Leviticus will strengthen our lives, so that we can grow as newborn babes, though we may have received Christ years ago.

The feasts are symbolic of times we spend communing with Christ, as a bride being betrothed to her husband. A covenant has been enacted , but the consummation of the relationship has yet to take place. If we do not have intimate fellowship with Christ, we can not learn Him. The Greek transliteration of the word fellowship is "Koinonia." It is very close in meaning to our English word commensality (the habit of eating together at the same table). Revelation 3:16 says, "If any man opens the door, I will come in, and I will sup with Him, and he with Me." This is the way I envision the feasts of the Lord. Jesus is standing at the door, the threshold of our hearts, and asking if He can come in and set up His dwelling-place with us! Then He invites us to set up our dwelling-place with Him! As we view these feasts we will find that many born-again, Spirit-filled saints are not keeping the feasts of the Lord in a spiritual sense. Therefore many are not maturing in Christ as they ought to be. They are not preparing to consummate a relationship with Jesus Christ!

Just as a child is nourished in the natural, and the diet of that child is conducive to its maturity, so likewise the believer in Christ must be nourished in each stage of life by the Holy Spirit's divine work.

The feasts mention our consecration to God as a progression of entering into the rest of the Lord. Surely there is a need for God's rest to come upon the church of Jesus Christ. In the modern society we live, we are often confronted with the stress and worry of daily living, where great demands are placed on us for performance and productivity. Even the church can become a "whirlpool of activity" oftentimes weakening instead of strengthening our relationship with God. Each feast explains how we can become closer to God in our relationship.

While we will review all of the feasts, this particular book has been written to examine and observe one of the solemn assemblies commanded by God called the Year of Jubilee.

Though as Christians, we are not under the old covenant, the Old Testament can serve as a shadow and type in strengthening our relationship with Christ.

As we study the Year of Jubilee, we can see how Christ is preparing us for the glory and splendor predestined for His bride. It will also help us to understand prophetically how God Almighty is dealing with His creation in this moment in which we now live. As we closed the twentieth century, we heard so much on preparing for Y2K. That dealt with the computer system's projected difficulty in translating the transition into numeric and algebraic format. But when God sends us through the transitions of life in His time it will translate people from the kingdom of darkness to the Kingdom of light. This process will take the acting of God's mighty hand.

The word Jubilee comes from a Hebrew transliteration word, "truwah", pronounced ter-oo-aw, which means *"trumpet, or clamor, i.e. acclamation of joy or a battle cry."* It is first mentioned in Leviticus 25:9. The following verses utilize a different Hebrew transliteration of jubilee, " yobel," meaning *"the blast of a horn (from it's continuous sound); spec. the signal of the silver trumpets; hence the instrument itself and the festival thus introduced: jubilee, ram's horn, trumpet."*

This year of Jubilee was celebrated by the blowing of a ram's horn to declare a time of liberation and celebration for God's people. It was blown on the day of atonement throughout all the land.

What this means to us is a splendid revelation of God's intended purpose to complete His work in the church. It is so breathtaking that we can by no means consume all of the knowledge in this short booklet. However, we will unfold the significance of this celebration to give you a better view of God's great grace He has shared with us through Christ in the coming chapters. First let's examine this time called "preparation."

Are you prepared to sound "yobel"? Everyone has a trumpet to blow. Everyone has an instrument that needs to be in tune with God. Are we really ready for the awesomeness a time of Jubilee brings to the church? I believe there is a purposeful order of the feasts.

The year of Jubilee is the last of the feasts mentioned, so there is much preparation to be done. Can I determine my place of preparation? If I am lacking in anything in which I need to be prepared, my prayer is, "Lord, prepare me!" Many of us in the church want to hurry up and get where we are going in God. We would rather hear the word "It is finished!" and "You are ready!" rather than "Wait on the Lord!" God is not going to stop working on the church until we come into a full knowledge of our position in Christ. There is a great call upon the church to come into a supernatural understanding of its relationship with Christ. The feasts depict the pursuit of man to come to a place where the supernatural can take precedence in our lives. I do believe there is, and has been for quite a while, a sense of urgency upon the church to get prepared to walk in a newness that brings a fresh aroma to those who see Christ in us. The time of preparation has always been important in God's dealings with His people. It is even more important now!

In order for us to understand the year of Jubilee, we must first began by looking at the sequence of the feasts listed in Leviticus, chapter 23.

Lev. chapter 23:1 declares, *"And the Lord spoke to Moses, saying, "**Speak to the children of Israel**, and say to them: 'The feasts of the Lord, which you shall proclaim to be holy convocations, these are My feasts.'"*

In other words, *"These feasts or times of assembly were not allocated by you, but I am the one who set these times apart in order that you may consecrate yourself for My purpose."*

That's what Jesus is speaking to us by revelation of the rhema word of God in this Old Testament verse. Even in historic times, it was God who set the feasts and the feasts belonged to God. We must have an understanding that coming to church is not man's idea, no more than salvation is man's idea. However, today it is our choice whether we will go to church or not! Men have always had a free will. The Bible tells us in Proverbs 16:1, "The preparation of the heart belongs unto men, but the answer of the tongue is from the Lord." While we will not venture too much into the numeric mentioned here, I think it is important to know that there are six feasts before we enter the year of Jubilee. Symbolically, "six" is the number of man (see Revelations 13:18), and it is in our understanding and preparing our hearts for these feasts that cause us to enter a time of Jubilee.

"Well, pastor, can't I prepare my heart without going to church? After all, the church is only a building! I can get this at home!"

My reasoning to you is so are all other places you go! You will find that it is not the place, but your face in the place that makes the difference. It is not just the building, however, but the purpose for the building. Let any business have no one to show up for work, and see if they are affected and if they accomplish their mission. The church is where much of God's business is initiated in our world. If everyone had that attitude, we would never get anything done for Jesus, no matter how much we know or love Him! You will see more clearly why we must be prepared to do the work of the kingdom of God as we go on. There is a time and a season for all things. These are some times we need to consider when we are preparing for Jubilee! All of these were designated times for Israel. We need to learn to designate time in our lives for the things God has ordained for our lives.

*1. It starts by reminding us to keep **the Sabbath** holy by having a solemn rest on the seventh day of every week. (A time of total repentance)*

Just as God rested on the seventh day after creating the world and all in it, we also must rest from our labor. Typically, the church observes this day of rest on Sunday, the first day of the week, in remembrance of Christ rising from the dead. This day is referred to as the Lord's day in the New Testament. The Jewish community observe the Sabbath on Saturday, the seventh day of the week according to the Pentateuch and historic customs. Man's natural need to cease from his labor, and rejuvenate his body is relative to his need to cease from all human efforts to reach God in his own strength. Though man may be sorry in his behavior toward God, as long as he continues in the same path, he will practice the same sin. For this reason, Sabbath is a type of repentance. Repentance is the act of turning to God, and turning away from sin.

The number "seven" is for perfection, so our repentance should be exact and precise in our approach to God. Before we experience salvation, we must first repent. There is no true redemption in human activity alone. However, we can present ourselves to God to be active in His divine plan in the earth.

Although, going to church does not redeem us, the Sabbath represents the act of coming to God's house as an opportunity to offer *repentance toward God.* This allows Him to show us His way of life in Christ.

Also, we live in a time where many people have access to the Gospel in various ways. However, I still believe that the great commission is to reap a harvest of souls which naturally manifest themselves in the gathering of local churches. Caught fish must be brought into the boat, therefore, a lost soul caught or won for Jesus Christ should be brought into the fellowship of the saints, and the saints are encouraged to come together. *"Not forsaking the assembling of yourselves together, as is the manner of some..." (Hebrews 10:25)*

Many times the final work of repentance will not happen until we can redirect the footsteps of that lost soul out of the world into the house of God.

John, the Baptist, spoke as a voice crying out in the wilderness to the Jews before Jesus came; *"Repent, for the kingdom of heaven is at hand!" (Matthew 3:2).* That is why the first feast to be kept is to observe the Sabbath. The feast of the Sabbath is our first recognition that we are dependent upon someone greater in strength than we are, and we need that someone to help us to be delivered from our own way of doing things.

The kingdom of God is learning how to do things like Jesus would do them.

Now what should we learn once we have came to the house of God to keep the first feast? I have decided that I don't want to continue the way I am! I have offered myself! There is a time and a season for all things. Before the time of Jubilee, there must be a time of true repentance. However, I must go further than the front door of the church, and I must go deeper in my relationship than the baptismal pool. I must keep the rest of the feasts!

*2. The **Passover** is the second feast mentioned as a commemoration of the Israelites being delivered from the bondage of Egypt when God smote the first born in Exodus chapter 12. (A time of redemption)*

Sin leaves an awful mess in our lives. Its marks go deeper than the surface of what people see. Sometimes people who are close to you will see just a glimpse of your imperfection and that's enough for them to pass their judgment upon you. But God knows everything about you. He knows even your secret faults and yet He loves you.

Each man was required to take a lamb for his house and place blood on the two door post and on the lintel of the house to protect themselves and their families when the angel of the Lord passed through the land. Whenever the angel of the Lord saw the blood, death passed over that house, thus it is called Passover.

The symbolism here is that Jesus Christ is the Lamb of God that atones for us and redeems us from the penalty of sin which is death. As John the Baptist declared, "Behold the Lamb that takes away the sins of the world." (John 1:29) Though we repent, we need something strong enough to save us. That something is the blood that came from Jesus. The bible tells us that without the shedding of blood, there can be no remission of sin. (Hebrews 9:14-15; Hebrews 13:12)

Who can we go to when we are looking for this power to rid us of all the regrets of our past, to erase all of the stains of our guilt, to eradicate all of the debt we may feel we owe humanity? Only Jesus has paid a high enough price to purchase all of the above. This spiritual purchase is so exemplified in the Passover. When the angel of death saw the blood, he passed over that house and the plague of death was cancelled. In the new covenant, the blood is the propitiation for our sins because " For the wages of sin is death…" (Romans 6:23a) . In other words we are earning our way to eternal damnation when we sin against God. If God gave us what we deserved we would all suffer death. "…but the gift of God is eternal life in Christ Jesus our Lord." (Romans 6:23b). But God's mercy and loving kindness continues to be extended to man. I have the blood of Jesus to thank for that.

> **3.** The **Feast of Unleavened Bread** *was observed for seven days after the Passover with a burnt offering. (A time of sanctification)*

"And He shall make a complete offering for sin." No work was done on these days which symbolizes our need of cleansing from sin. Jesus Christ came to bear our iniquities, and redeem us from sin. The unleavened bread is two-fold in its meaning .

First of all, the unleavened bread symbolizes our holy nature in Christ apart from sin. We must first acknowledge we are sinners before we can fully understand redemption. However, we must see ourselves as perfect in Christ once we are redeemed. Thus the number of days is seven symbolizing perfection. Jesus said, "Be ye holy, for I am Holy." Our sanctification is the act of appropriating the righteousness of God in our lives. Without salvation, even the year of Jubilee is not fully comprehended because God is speaking to us once we have already experienced the other feasts. It is also the case with sanctification. So if you haven't received Jesus Christ as your personal Savior, that is a feast you have not kept.

Secondly, it symbolizes Jesus Christ as our sin offering. "He who knew no sin became sin for us that we might become the righteousness of God in Christ Jesus."- 2 Corinthians 5:21 . The only way for me to receive salvation in Christ's redemption by which He died for the whole world (John 3:16) is to acknowledge my need for a Savior! I can believe that Jesus paid it all, but I must believe He paid it all for me to be saved from my sins!

Jesus offered Himself once for sin forever. He gave His life for my sins and yours. We must be reminded of Christ's willingness to be broken like unleavened bread, and make sure we are not soon shaken in our position of faith in God. It is called sins, not sin; transgressions, not iniquities. Even though we have already repented, we are now redeemed by the blood for the remission of our sins. Reconciliation has already occurred and will continue in our lives through sanctification. Sanctification comes by the word of reconciliation given to us. It is a work continued in a believer's life once Jesus comes into the heart.

"You are already clean because of the word which I have spoken to you." (John 15:3)

"Sanctify them through your word for your word is truth." (John 17:17)

> **4.** *The **Feast of Pentecost**, also called the **Feast of Weeks** and **Feast of First Fruits** was a time of harvest in which the people gave thanks to God for the bountifulness by which He had blessed them.*

Our bountiful blessing came on the day of Pentecost in Acts, chapter 2, as Joel chapter 2 prophesies the Spirit of the Lord being poured out on all flesh. <u>The baptism of the Holy Spirit is an integral part of our growth, maturity, and empowerment in Christ.</u> Once saved, Jesus orchestrates our lives from the throne of our hearts to bring us closer to Him. The Holy Spirit causes us to be sensitive not only to His "woos", but also to His "woes". Jesus wants us to know Him not only as Savior, but also as Lord.

The Feast of Pentecost also represents the sacrifice of our service. The word, "Pentekostos", in Greek transliteration is an adjective for fiftieth, which is the fiftieth day after Passover, counting from the second day of the Feast. It is during this time that Israel was to bring their first fruits to the Lord.

All that they presented was to be "holy to the Lord for the priests." (Leviticus 23:16-20)

We should be willing to sacrifice our time in service to the Lord also. We may not be offering seven lambs, and one bullock and two rams, but our offering is still a sacrifice. We bring the sacrifice of our thanksgiving to God into the house of the Lord through praise and worship. We will discuss this further as we go into other chapters of this book.

> **5.** *The* **Feast of Trumpets** *highlighted the entrance into the Day of Atonement with a memorial of blowing trumpets on the first of the seventh month.*
> *(A time of reconciliation)*

The words atonement and reconciliation is used synonymously in our reference to Scripture. It comes from the Greek transliteration, "kattalage" which deals specifically with the releasing of a debt that one must pay. It explains our position in Christ once we are saved. We are removed from our debt to serve sin because the wages of sin is death. Once we serve sin, it causes us to become a debtor to serve it, because it is a debt we can never pay. But once we become "born again", we are totally cleared from our debt to sin and we are now free to serve Jesus Christ. Remember this scripture: "Therefore if any man be in Christ Jesus, He is a new creature, old things are passed away, and behold all things are become new." (2 Corinthians 5:17).

Once we come to know Christ, we no longer have to keep paying our former landlord, the devil! We have moved from his condemned premises to God's blessed premises, and from his broken promises to God's covenant promises.

Ten days later, the Day of Atonement was observed as the people afflicted their souls and gave burnt offerings to God for the remission of their sins. We find here that God is calling His people back for a time of seeking His face. Why are they seeking His face? Here the emphasis is not necessarily on our sin nature, but acts of transgression against God, both knowingly and unknowingly. Ten is the number of testing, but after the test, we will have a testimony. This was a memorial service. You can not remember something you've never known.

God wants us to have a story to tell, not about our history, but about His-story of redeeming us from our sins! We must evangelize our world with the message of atonement. Paul said in 2 Corinthians 5:20 that *"God has given US the word of reconciliation."* Revelations 12 says *"they overcame him (the devil) by the word of their **testimony**..."* The trumpet is our testimony. Blowing the trumpet is symbolic of spreading the good news through proclaiming, preaching, declaring and broadcasting the Word of

God to those who need to know Him. "*Go ye into all the world, and preach the gospel...*" (Mark 16:15) You may not tell it like I tell it, but you have a testimony. Go and tell it!

"*So then faith comes by hearing, and hearing by the word of God." (Romans 10:17 NKJV)*

"*Therefore if any man be in Christ Jesus, He is a new creation, old things are passed away, and behold all things are become new. And you have received the word of reconciliation." (2 Corinthians 5:17, 19)*

The Scriptures say that no one can come to God, unless the Holy Spirit draws him. The Holy Spirit often draws us through the sound of God's Word. The blowing of the trumpet symbolizes the proclamation of God's Word in the midst of our circumstances that cause us to come to a place of repentance in order to experience the continuance of atonement or reconciliation as it is shared with those who yet do not know Him. True reconciliation is bringing back the fervor of our relationship to God through the love of Jesus Christ. The extension of that reconciliation will effectively work in our lives as we relate to one another. Many times in the church, we have attempted to put the carriage before the horse. We want reconciliation on our terms when true reconciliation is God working in us on His terms.

Evangelism is God's solution to man's dilemma. Many times we forget to evangelize the heart before we deal with the soul. An unredeemed heart can never understand the things of God! We must reach the heart first, because that is where the issues lie. (Proverbs 4:23; Matthew 15:18-20)

*6. Our experience should then progress to **the Feast of Tabernacles** where we are <u>established in the house of the Lord</u> to do the work of the ministry.
(A time of establishment)*

Many of us have come through the door, but we haven't entered into the house yet. There are many rooms in God's house. We have been baptized in the Holy Ghost, but unlike the Old Testament saints, we have not chosen a trade, availed our gifts, been equipped with a skill in the house of the Lord. We may be doing many things, but are we dedicated to the Lord. One particular thing I love about this feast is it is an extension into **the Sabbath year**. In other words, it does imply that we, as children of God, must go beyond an inconsistent life of "sometime living." Here the emphasis is on a year, not a day!

In the Sabbath year, Israel was to give the land rest by neither sowing their fields nor pruning their vineyards. They were instructed to eat the produce from the field. So the supply didn't come from their own labor, but by seeds already planted which are able to bear fruit. The only thing that truly counts to God are the spiritual produce of the Holy Spirit already sown into your life. Over the years, God has made a rich investment in the saints of God. This symbolizes years of dedication in serving the Lord in a true sense of worship in the Spirit of the Lord! These saints represent those who continued in the house of the Lord, and served faithfully.

*I believe the Lord Jesus Christ's ultimate will is not only to do a redemptive work in bringing in a harvest of souls, but His great pleasure is to reward **those who have served faithfully in the house of God**. I believe this with all my heart!*

What is the Father in His awesome plan preparing us for? What awaits us in this time called ***Jubilee***? Though we have discussed some wonderful things, the best is yet to come!

CHAPTER 3

WHAT IS JUBILEE?

The **Year of Jubilee** was celebrated at a notable time. All of the above mentioned feasts prepares for the magnificent outcome we are about to unfold. Only after seven cycles of seven years of celebrating the Sabbath, did the people of God experience jubilee. Remember also that this is the seventh festival Israel is told to observe! Seven is the number of perfection! Jesus wants to perfect the Church! This would bring them to the fiftieth year when God would specify the ordinance to be kept in the Year of Jubilee. Five multiplied by ten is fifty. In the Scriptures, five is the number for grace, and ten is the number for testimony or testament. Therefore, *jubilee* is a time when God will perfect the *testimony* of *grace* in our lives. What is grace. " The divine influence upon the heart to do good." (Vine's Expository Dictionary of old testament and new testament words;) It is the Lord moving upon man to act in a way of divine favor.

God's grace magnified is my life glorified! I need God's grace to make it.

As I said before, the blessing of Jubilee will be much more glorious in its unfolding, depending on how we perceive it. Here we will examine the great blessings that are awaiting us in the years ahead! What feast are you in at this present moment? Are you still in one of the previous six feasts we mentioned? If so, remember you are on God's time clock, and, yes, your time is coming!

As we mentioned in our introduction, the word Jubilee comes from a Hebrew transliteration word, "truwah", pronounced ter-oo-aw, which means *"trumpet, or clamor, i.e. acclamation of joy or a battle cry."* It is first mentioned in Leviticus 25:9. The following verses after Leviticus 25:9 utilize a different Hebrew transliteration of jubilee, " yobel", meaning *"the blast of a horn (from it's continuous sound); spec. the signal of the silver trumpets; hence the instrument itself and the festival thus introduced: jubilee, ram's horn, trumpet."*

The trumpet remains a powerful symbol of God's voice in the midst of His people and will serve as a landmark as we unfold the significance of the year of Jubilee. Also remember that the color silver is symbolic of redemption. That means the call of festive gathering is for a redeemed people, namely the children of God. "The Trumpet" is indeed blowing in Zion, admonishing the saints to enter into a place of fellowship with Christ that causes us to be that renowned people that display the greatness and strength of God in Jesus Christ. The Lord still utters His voice before His army, the church of Jesus Christ.

Jesus said in Luke 4:18, *"The Spirit of The Lord is upon Me, because He has anointed Me to preach the gospel to the poor, He has sent Me to heal the brokenhearted, to preach deliverance to the captives and the recovery of sight to the blind, to set at liberty those who are oppressed, to preach the acceptable year of the Lord."*

> Jesus has a message for poor people!
>
> Jesus has a message for hurting people!
>
> Jesus has a message for imprisoned people!
>
> Jesus has a message for lost people!
>
> Jesus has a message for oppressed people!
>
> We need to preach the message Jesus preached!

Jesus has released His message to us through the preaching of the Word of God. As there are a variety of ways in which God speaks to us:

1. *God's prophetic voice* is proclaiming His purpose and destiny like the sound of the trumpet.

2. *God's evangelistic voice* is declaring redemption to all who will receive Jesus as Savior.

3. *God's instructional voice* is teaching us to bring our lives in line with the will of God.

4. *God's nurturing voice* helps us to grow spiritually in Christ in our local settings on a daily basis.

5. *God's directional voice* is clarifying the move of the Holy Spirit in the church to bring forth an established work!

Behold, the manifold wisdom of God!

The Lord is sounding the trumpet in these days to awaken us to the purposes of God in our lives! That's why the trumpet is blowing! We are being called by the Lord to be equipped as the mighty army of the Lord. We are like valiant soldiers on a mission with our God. That's why we must be ready, even before "ready" gets ready, we need to be ready! That's why we must examine where we are, so we can know where we are going!

In the Sabbath year, Israel was to give the land rest by neither sowing its fields nor pruning its vineyards. Depending on what type of struggle you may have had in life, this rest can take you from one phase of glory to another phase of glory. They were instructed to eat the produce from the field. While this is true also in the fiftieth year of Jubilee, there was a proclamation given by the blowing of the trumpet throughout the land which set all the people free who were in slave to labor in order to bring forth crop. It became a year of reaping for everyone. Israel's requirement to set all of its slaves free and to allow everyone to return to his own house to his own family is a symbol of God's great grace in the Lord Jesus Christ setting us free from the enslavement of sin, and returning us to the household of faith and the family of God thereby bringing wholeness to each individual. There are three basic ordinances in the year of Jubilee:

1. A time of rest for God's people and the soil of the land. (Leviticus 25:11).
2. A time to restore all distribution of land back to the original owner.
3. Every Israelite who sold himself because of poverty and could not redeem himself was set free **along with his children**.

In other words, God wiped their slates clean and everyone now had a chance to begin again with a new start. We were given a new start when we first came to Jesus and asked that our sins be forgiven. In order for this time of jubilee to happen, the Lord Jesus is going to have to do some serious pardoning of sins and restoring of broken lives, and He is willing to do just that!

"If any man be in Christ, he is a new creation: old things have passed away, and behold all things are become new."
(2 Corinthians 5:17)

In Lev. 25:17-18, we read, "Therefore,

1. you shall not oppress one another, but
2. you shall fear your God; for I am the Lord your God...
3. you shall observe My statutes and
4. keep My judgments, and
5. perform them; and
6. you will dwell in the land in safety."

These six charges to the people of Israel help us to see that God's interest is to progressively bring about a change in the spiritual condition of those who serve Him. They were already serving Him, however it is clear that the system of order they had personally adopted was interfering with the divine order God himself desires for His people.

Sometimes we can have great order in our lives, and still have no time for God! I believe we are far from finding out the ways of God, and only a time of jubilee in the church will bring about the kind of glory Christ is still unfolding to the church. This particular verse of scripture in Leviticus 25:18-19 expounds on God's great concern in giving us the liberty of the Holy Spirit to fulfill our worship towards Him without interference of social, political, economical, and even spiritual bondage within and without the walls of the local church. In fact, it is often the influence of this bondage that causes the glory of Christ *not* to manifest in the life of the believer in the way that it should. We are indeed *oppressed* in many ways by the very things we have prioritized as important in our own lives. We give so much time to these things that we lose sight of what is truly a priority to God.

The liberation of the Holy Spirit is very important in ones life. Without it there are no free will offerings, without it there is no willing mind, without it there is no cheerful heart, for there is no joy in bondage. In order to learn more about God's purpose for liberation, we will devote a chapter entirely to this subject. Though we have come to understand a degree of divine order; respect for authority, tithing, leadership training and ordination, liturgical order of bishop, honoring our pastors and so forth and so on, we need to view divine order as fulfilling God's plans, not our own. the *superficial nature* of our knowledge, and often *premature assumptions* lead to even greater bondage than we had before we received the knowledge.

John 8:36, declares, *"Therefore, if the Son makes you free, you shall be free indeed."* If it is truly the Lord, the end result will be liberty in Christ. I believe there are moments in the church that we must sit down, and think about where we are going, and ask the Lord if we are really pleasing Him, or if we are only interested in our own successes. If your success is producing more bondage, instead of setting people free, you really need to consider your ministry to Jesus.

- Whenever a trumpet sounds, it must sound for a purpose.
- It must be clear and distinct, so that people know what to do (1 Corinthians 14:4,5).

The trumpet must be distinct in order to tell us whether it is a time of rejoicing, or a time for battle. The trumpet is declaring, "Children of God, it's time for Jubilee." Just as Moses sounded the trumpet for the movement of the camp of Israel, so Jesus is calling us, His church, to a higher place in Him.

- Do we know what He is calling us to be, to become, and to do?
- What are the spiritual things that mark the life of one who lives in the liberty of the Holy Spirit? (2 Corinthians 3:17).
- What is the Lord Jesus, our King of kings and Lord of lords declaring for His Kingdom?
- What is the significance in the sound of the trumpet?

In the following chapters, we will discover what the trumpet call is in the year of Jubilee, and why we must yield to the Holy Spirit for an awesome work of this magnitude to take place in the church of the living God. We must go on to perfection in Christ, and grow up from being children to being full grown in the kingdom of God! We must resound, not only the praises of God from our lips, but also the victory we must walk in Christ to fulfill His will and destiny. Let's hear what the trumpet is saying to us in these precious extensions of eternity we call time! What time is it for the church? What are the most valuable gifts we have that we need to cherish to let God arise in our lives?

CHAPTER 4

THE TRUMPET CALL TO PRAYER

"PRAYING WITH ALL PRAYER AND SUPPLICATION IN THE SPIRIT..."
(EPHESIANS 6:18-A)

The trumpet blasted to gather a solemn assembly. A people focused on Jesus and His purpose. A holy convocation immediately conversed on Mount Zion. It was not only a time to proclaim, but a time to pray. I can imagine there were all kinds of people gathering as the trumpet sounded. I am sure it was not a convenient time for each of them, therefore sacrifices had to be made. Prayer is a sacrifice yet its rewards are eternal. *"The effectual fervent prayer of a righteous man availeth much."* (James 5:16b KJV)

The Lord Jesus revealed this to me in such an exciting way through the scriptures! How do we obtain the peace of God in our lives, especially in a world filled with uncertainty? Jesus, Himself, forewarned us it would be this way in the last days.

2 Timothy 3:1-7 tells us the state of the end times declaring, *"But mark this: there will be <u>terrible</u> <u>times</u> in the last days. People will be lovers of themselves, lovers of money, boastful, proud, abusive,*

disobedient to parents, ungrateful, unholy, without love, unforgiving, slanderous, without self-control, brutal, not lovers of good, treacherous, rash, conceited, lovers of pleasure rather than lovers of God- having a form of godliness but denying it's power. Have nothing to do with them. They are the ones who worm their way into the houses of weak-willed women, who are loaded down with sins and are swayed by all kinds of evil desires., always learning, but never able to acknowledge the truth."

We must realize that we, as the people of God, have lost our focus on Christ! Do not get caught up in the troubles of our day. An alarm must be sounded in order to awaken us to the glory of this Final Hour! The year of Jubilee cannot be fulfilled without the solemnity among the people. Solemnity simply means peace. Having peace is not a word thing, but a state of being. Peace is a result of resolution to internal and external conflicts.

Though there are trying times around us we can still have the peace of God. Prayer is our help in God. Prayer helps us to resolve matters without natural aid and then teaches us how to become resourceful with the natural aid God gives us. The time of jubilee must be a time of prayer.

We should continue to hear the call of God and strive to be found in Christ during this time of great unrest in the lives of people. We ought to be lifting up holy hands, without wrath or doubting, praying for the Holy Spirit to truly guide us in this hour!

Paul quoted these words to the church at Philippi, *"Be anxious for nothing, but in everything through prayer, and supplication with thanksgiving, let your request be made known unto God."*- Philippians 3:6. He was speaking to them concerning internal, as well as external conflicts.

How do we gather a solemn assembly? How do we enter into this rest that the year of Jubilee proclaims? What do we do with all the unsettled issues in our lives? While the above verse is simple in syntax, it holds a great key to our lesson on the peace of God. Let's review this scripture to get more wisdom from God on this matter.

1. "Be anxious for nothing...", Paul says! We must first get rid of all the worry so we can rest in the Lord.

Stress is still the number one killer in our society, because it leads to heart disease. Jubilee is a time of peace. You need rest from stress! Many of us need the peace of God in our lives. We have many who have sleepless nights, and many who experience great depression, no matter what state the economy is in.

"Don't Worry!!!" The Scripture says, God gives His beloved sleep. Jesus wants to bring His Church, the bride of Christ into a place of rest. You may say, "Lord Jesus, if I could rid myself of this excessive worry, I would be free in my service toward you." Yet we are often busy serving Him with our worries. The problem with the church today is she is too anxious in activity oftentimes without seeking God in a time of consecrated prayer. Anxiety is nothing more than "worry in motion." Jesus does not want His bride to be worried! I am not able to relax if my wife is not re-laxed! When things are not settled around my home with her, I am also unsettled. That is just a natural thing! We say to our-selves, "I can't just sit here, I must do something", when the something we need to do is pray. We always can find a reason why we need to 'help God out'. How quickly we forget that God does not need "out", because He never had the problem! You did. You need the help, not God! We cannot rid ourselves of it. We simply hand it over to the Lord, and let Him handle it! We must realize there are times things are out of our control. However, the Lord Jesus is always in control. We must learn to trust in Him.

It is easier for most people to work than to rest, but God's remedy in many of our problems lie in the ability God gave Israel at the Red Sea. Just as He told Moses, *" Stand still, and see the salvation of the Lord,"* this is what He is saying to you.

2. Once we come into the rest of the Lord, we can offer Him pure prayer.

Philippians 4:6 goes on to say, "...but in everything through prayer and supplication...". **Prayer** is the beckoning of God's power to operate on our behalf according to our petition we desire of Him.

Prayer is always a key to our resting in God. Notice here that Paul the apostle speaks of prayer "in everything", that is, for every circumstance.

No matter what we face, God is able to bring us through it all. You can always depend on Him. You can believe that when you go to Him to get an answer, He is already waiting to do His mighty act in your life. That's a guarantee!

Supplication is also important. When we bring supplication to God, we articulate our dependency by acknowledging we are confident in coming to Him for all the things we believe He is able to do and to be. Supplication connects us back to the source of our supply, and reminds us of the awesome and wonderful character God has granted us in Jesus Christ. We need the supply of the Holy Spirit just to walk with Jesus everyday.

Prayer is asking for God's hand to work on our behalf. I have found over the years when I pray, the Lord also uncovers the work of my enemies who are working against me. Though we can not defend ourselves at all times in the flesh, the Lord Jesus is a banner of victory in every situation we may face in life. So you need not spend time worrying about those who are against you. You must remain focused on God.

Just keep praying even when you can not see the obvious answer. You will see God move on your behalf. Hallelujah!

3. The verse continues by saying *"with thanksgiving"*

We may not always feel thankful in the moment. I know what it means to have a bad day, a bad week, and just a difficult time. But life in motion needs a time of meditation. Finding this time to take a short breath and to just be thankful is like medicine to the soul.

However it may take more to resolve the often unpredictable twists and unsuspected turns of your day. That's when we need to do more than recline in the chair for a nap. This may call for bringing into your remembrance the goodness of the Lord in your life.

A session of prayers will lead us into a position of adoration and *thanksgiving to Jesus* for what He has done, what He is doing, and what He will do.

Acknowledge Him in all His attributes. Think upon His greatness. Rest upon His faithfulness. This will bring the peace of God into your life.

4. The verse finally concludes by saying, "Let your request be made known to God."

It is not your need God does not know about, but whether or not you desire the need to be met.

Jesus said, *"... for My heavenly Father knows the things you need before you ask."* He goes on to explain, *"Ask, and it shall be given; seek, and you shall find; knock, and the door shall be opened to you."*

God already knows your needs. He simply needs a record of your request in Heaven (1 John 5:13-15).

A request is like taking an order at a restaurant. If you don't place an order, you will not be served! Often we are waiting for the Lord to meet our needs, while He is waiting to take our order. That is what a request is. It is your Heavenly order you have placed with your Father in Heaven. Yes, the Father knows what you need. However, you may need some patience while you wait until he lets you know it is done. When it is time, He will let you know by coming to the table where you are still in fellowship with Him. Are you keeping the feast of the Lord? Are you coming to a place where the table is set to hear the Word of God? You must also see Him as the porter or the waiter. If the Lord is coming to serve your blessing he needs to know what table you are sitting. If He does not know, it is like the mailman trying to find your mailbox and you do not even have an address. When He is finally done, He will say, "Your order is ready!"

The Bible says, *"Call to Me, and I will answer you and show you great and mighty things, which you do not know."* (Jeremiah

33:3) God wants to hear me pray to Him. Just as the bugle awakens the soldier to arise and fulfill duty, prayer must be a duty; a necessity I must fulfill in my life. David said,

"O God, You are my God; early will I seek You; my soul thirsts for You; my flesh longs for You in a dry and thirsty land where there is no water". (Psalm 63:1)

I make God happy when I approach Him in prayer. Prayer aligns my life in such a way that I am thankful to God in all of life's circumstances! Don't allow the enemy to get you out of line with the will of God in your praying. Keep praying, believing you will have it! Thank Him for the answer before you see it!

The trumpet that is blowing in the church is a beseeching that our hearts will bow when our knees are bent; our souls will break open as our lips are parted; and that our minds will focus on the glory of God in Jesus Christ as our hands are folded.

Pray! Pray in all types of ways until you know you have communicated effectively to the Heavenly Father in Jesus Name. Pray in such a way that the Holy Spirit is revealing to God the great depth of your needs and desires in life. That is the call of God upon each of our lives. Many times we struggle in life because we forget to pray. Prayer releases us from our troubles so that we can live for God.

CHAPTER 5

THE TRUMPET CALL TO PRAISE

"FOR OUT OF THE MOUTHS OF BABES AND INFANTS
YOU HAVE PERFECTED PRAISE."
(PSALMS 9:2)

The year of Jubilee is a time to testify of God's goodness. Surely the Lord has been good to us all, however we are not always filled with gratitude because of His goodness. When we think gifts, many of us immediately think of gifts of the Holy Spirit. While these gifts are important, there are other gifts that the grace of God has measured out to every man and it is unlimited what God will do when we utilize these gifts.

1. Praise is a unique gift God has given to mankind.

In other words, praise is something everyone can do (Psalms 150:1). The perfection of praise, however is reserved for the children of God, who serve the Lord Jesus In presenting themselves as an offering of praise to God (1 Peter 2:7).

Jubilee festivals always presented the best in praise. The trumpets resounded with all the instruments in harmony and melody. Everyone presented their gifts to bring praise to the Lord. The praises of God were made glorious.

"Make a joyful noise unto the Lord, all ye lands. Serve the Lord with gladness: come before His presence with singing. Know ye that the Lord, He is our God. It is He who hath made us and not we ourselves: we are His people and the sheep of His pasture. Come into His gates with thanksgiving and enter His courts with praise; be thankful unto Him, and bless His name. For the Lord is good, and His mercy endureth forever, and His truth endureth to all generations." (Psalm 100 KJV)

That's what God wants to do in this time of Jubilee in our lives.

"Make His praise glorious!"
"Praise is comely to the upright!"
"Hallelujah!"

2. Christ must still remain in the center stage of our praise.

Praise is not entertainment, no matter how excellent or elegant the noise is we hear. Thank God we have trained and skilled musicians that know how to produce and present music and song. We, the people of God, and those of us who are called to be saints, listen to so many Gospel artists today. We are so dramatic in our praise. However we must keep our focus.

Jesus must still remain the center of our praise- not Kirk Franklin; not BeBe Winan; not CeCe Winan; not Don Moen; not Commissioned; not Amy Grant; not Sandi Patty; not Martha Munizzi; not Fred Hammond; not Ron Kenoly; not Israel and New Breed. Though these singers are not all from the same generation or genre, praise should never lose its savor or flavor in Christ. These all simply become performers if our focus is not exalting Christ.

And besides these, there are many artists who are beginning to cross over from the secular music industry, still bringing their baggage with them (and they have not even started to unpack)! Yes we have some of this kind also. We read about them in our newspapers and magazines. Sometimes once it is known that there is an economic advantage and opportunity, you will have those who come who will have the wrong motives. However, Jesus Christ must still remain at the center stage of our praise! We must be open and trustworthy of what truly represents Him.

There is a trumpet call of praise that declares that praise will be perfected out of the mouth of babes (Psalm 8:2; Matthew 21:16)- those who are nourished by the Word of God, fed by the loving care of a tender mother. If God is our Father then we need to be nurtured from His Holy Word and keep hearing what He is saying through His church, the bride of Christ. There are some musical artists that need that time to nurture. It does not mean they should not make the transition from secular to gospel music. However there is a transformation that may need to truly be realized in the heart and mind that brings passion and true conviction to the song. I believe that we can still make the distinction between the lyrics, tunes, melodies, and character of what we sing to the Lord. I do not believe all music is the same. We should make a difference in the way we combine our talents, gifts, and skills to glorify God.

The church of Jesus Christ must stand in the gap during this hour of trial in the music and lyrics as we continue to pay tribute to the Lord Jesus Christ. If this indeed be the case, I believe the bride ought to know what her husband wants. The church is the bride of Christ, and she should stay at the center of measuring what is healthy and unhealthy for the children of God. We don't need to turn all this authority God has given us, His wife, over to a harlot, whether it be a Gospel promoter or a well renowned artist. All things may be expedient, but all things are not necessary.

Many who present praise today still have a great need to be nurtured themselves. When they have not yet submitted their lives to the Lord, it is not always so easy to hide this fact. Those who are hearing beyond just the music can discern the call for help. The artist may need to spend some time with God in making that transition from entertainment to bringing praise to God. There is an anointed call to genuine praise from the heart. If the praise we sing is not comely, pleasant to the heart and appreciated for it's graciousness to the upright (those who are striving to live their lives well-pleasing to God), then we should consider what we are singing.

We should always think in terms of pleasing Christ and His church. It matters how the people of God are affected by what we sing, whatever we are singing. Please, do not get me wrong here. There is not one of these musical artists that I have not listened to in my own Christian walk. In fact, those I have mentioned are some of my own favorites. But my personal preference does not censor anyone's music or song. The level of censorship I am talking about is a spiritual awakening we need desperately in our time in order to know what pleases God. Yes, it is still about what exalts, magnifies, and glorifies the Lord. That should be the pursuit and desire of every praise leader, musician, and recording artist who is named among the Name above all names, Jesus Christ.

3. Our mission ought to be perfecting and maturing our gifts, talents, and skills to bring glory to God in His Fullness in Jesus Christ- our praise.

The praise does not stop with the lips, but continues with the life. Are you connected with God? Are your gifts, talents and skills truly being used to exalt yourself or exalt the Lord? Are you willing to bring the sacrifice of praise into the house of the Lord? As we said before, the church is the bride of Christ in which every gift, talent and skill ca be nurtured and matured.

Our mission in life ought to be an instrument of praise, not in just our voices, but in our service to Him in our daily lives. Perfecting our lives to Christ will take more than a trip to the studio; it will take a lifetime journey with Jesus. Praise is a continuous adventure with Jesus. David said, *"I will bless the Lord at all times; His praise shall continually be in my mouth."* (Psalm 34:1) The Psalms also declares, *"Everyday will I bless you, and I will praise your name forever and ever ."* (Psalm 145:2)

There are three areas from which God can release praise from a vessel of God, and these three determine God's purpose for the vessel. These three are gifts, talents, and skills. I encourage those of you who are called to the ministry of music, praise, or the psalmist ministry to understand that the vessel must be willing to experience the fullness of God in all three dimensions to become most effective. However, praise is acceptable to God before it comes to maturity.

This should encourage many of you who are just beginning to walk in your call to allow God to minister through you where you are until you mature into that ministry. It should also encourage those who have matured to understand that even before you came to the point of where you are, the Lord was pleased with your praise. The Jubilee experience is not just a formal affair. It is a spontaneous gathering of God's people to collide in the praises of God from all walks of life. Praise must first be acceptable before it is perfected. God accepts all three, but the heart is what makes the three just one offering acceptable to God.

CHAPTER 6

THE TRUMPET CALL TO WORSHIP

"GOD IS A SPIRIT, AND THEY THAT WORSHIP HIM,
MUST WORSHIP HIM IN SPIRIT AND IN TRUTH."
(JOHN 4:24)

In worship, we acknowledge God for who He is, not for what He has done. As long as there are things hindering me from getting beyond the veil in my relationship with God, I can never enter into worship. Worship is in the Holy of Holies, where often words are not spoken, yet thoughts have been exchanged. Articulation is not always needed for transformation. Worship is a transforming experience.

Worship so fills the spirit that it must find an outlet to express its glory, to unveil its splendor, to reveal its beauty. Worship is something the bound soul cannot experience. That is why this trumpet of liberty must resound. This trumpet call is for the heart to be set free to roam into the inner courts, beyond the veil, and grip the mercy seat until the ark of covenant arises in the heart.

1. Worship is the expression of our appreciation to God in our daily activity.

Many songs we sing are praise in which we adore Him for what He has done, but in worship we adore Him for who He is among us and in us. We can perfect our praise, but in reality only the Spirit of the Lord can bring us into true worship. You can have great harmony, sing a wondrous melody, conduct a lovely rendition upon multiple instruments, but the thing that will bring the glory of God into our midst is the presence of God. Hallelujah!

Worship! That's the place where Jesus is closer to you than you are to yourself!

Worship! That's where the yokes are destroyed because of the anointing.

Worship! Authentic from the heart without fabrication; prepared, yet unrehearsed.

Worship!

2. Our worship is an extension of how we perceive God.

King David was a great example of a life of worship. The bible says that David was a man after God's own heart. This is where true worship starts. Psalm 91:1-2 says, "He that dwells in the secret place of the most High, shall abide under the shadow of the Almighty, I will say of the Lord, He is my refuge, and my fortress, my God, in Him will I trust." Though this whole verse of

scripture unveils the beauty of worship, the five final words, "…
in Him will I trust," bring an undeniable conclusion; *the Lord is
ultimately the consummation of all I can fathom as reliable, and
having complete integrity in providing all-sufficient care as I remain connected in Him.* This is what I perceive David is saying in
this verse of scripture. I must keep my heart connected with God,
because He is the only One who can defend me in all things.

We read about David, and we see that though he had a perfect
heart, he did not have a perfect life. Yet God was able to bring
him through all things, both good and bad. When we worship
God, we must be reminded that God is Faithful! This is a charac-
teristic of who God is, not what He has done. Worship helps us to
reflect God's faithfulness in our lives, in good and in bad times.
We can only reflect the part of God's character we truly know.
Even Jesus tells us this when He asked which man would be most
thankful, the man who is forgiven a little, or the man who is forgiven much. Surely the man who is forgiven much, but only if he
can first recognize how much he has been forgiven. Look around
you at all the churches you know. We worship God the way we
perceive Him. According to the measure of His goodness, we
measure out our goodness to others.

3. Our worship must be "up close and personal"!

Do I really know Him, or am I going only on what others have
told me about Him? I must know Him even as I am known. I
must get closer to Him. Just as a bride must remove the veil to
look her husband in the eyes, so I must look Jesus in the eyes to
know Him. I must see Him as He really is. I am speaking of personal relationship! Just as much as I know my wife, I must know

Jesus. Relationships do not grow overnight. We have to spend time with one another. Some of those times aren't spent on resorts, mountains, and counting seashells on the oceanfront. Some of those times are very difficult. They may be stressful, sorrowful, and disappointing unlike the gracious moments we love to experience so much. But these invested times help us to truly realize our deep love for one another. They sew within the fabric of our existence a powerful thread that can never be separated.

Worship entails all of these. The same way we learn to love our spouse more deeply we also learn how to love God more deeply. Paul, the apostle described it this way in Ephesians 3:17-19; "… that Christ may dwell in your hearts through faith; that you, being rooted and grounded in love may be able to comprehend with all the saints, what is the width and length and depth and height -- to know the love of Christ which passes knowledge; that you may be filled with all the fullness of God."

In Genesis 4:1, it says that Adam knew Eve, his wife. That word in Hebrew transliteration is "yadah"! Adam yadah Eve. That word yadah is dealing with the knowing that produces offspring, namely "intimate relationship that involves close and personal contact." That is how Jesus wants our worship to be toward Him; "up close and personal"!

4. Worship is the genuine extension of my life to God.

We have so many different ways we <u>want</u> to worship Jesus. There is the Methodist way. There is the Presbyterian way. There is the Catholic way. There is the Lutheran way. There is the Baptist way. There is the Pentecostal way. When Jesus dealt with the philosophy of the woman at the well in John 4:23. He explained the type of worship the Father expects from us:

"But the hour is coming , and now is , when the true worshipers will worship the Father in spirit and in truth; for the Father is seeking such to worship Him."

Worship is about knowing God. Everyone believes that their way is alright, but Jesus is still saying, "No one can come to Me unless the Father who sent Me draws him; and I will raise him up in the last day." (John 6:44) My worship must excel toward God, the Father through Jesus Christ by the anointing of the Holy Spirit. It must go from glory to glory, faith to faith, and grace to grace. For example, I can not believe in sovereign grace, and not believe in prevailing grace. I can not believe in prevailing grace and not believe in saving grace. I grow to understand the different types of graces because I encounter them at different stages of life. The Holy Spirit leads me to know more about His grace the same way He teaches me to know about worship! Grace helps me to know God for who He truly is.

Whatever the Holy Spirit draws me into as the truth of God's word in my life, that's what I am willing to walk in! "Sanctify them through your Word, your Word is truth." (John 17:17)

CHAPTER 7

THE TRUMPET CALL OF UNITY

"BEHOLD HOW GOOD AND PLEASANT IT IS FOR BRETHREN
TO DWELL TOGETHER IN UNITY!"
(PSALM 133:1)

Unity is one of those things you hear much about these days. Our world is possessed with "bywords" and "slogans" that can really tickle the ears, and make us really feel warm inside. Sometimes we can become carried away in the acoustics of outward displays and forget the foundation that causes those things to be established in our lives. I learned not to become too excited over lip service anymore. I've found that many of my life's blessings did not come from those I expected, but from those God ordained. I went to many conferences trying to find where I could fit in the body of Christ. I received prophetic blessings from some profound and respected men of God in the body of Christ, but the true essence of unity did not lie in any of the ascetic worship services I attended, nor the great men and women I met. Because my heart longed for unity so greatly, I was often disappointed with my experiences, and many times my prophetic insight allowed me to see through many "smokescreens" and "glass houses". Then the Lord led my wife and I to Abundant Life Church of Christ in Richmond, Virginia. There we found love, acceptance, friendship, and a fathering heart in Pastor Steve Foreman. We also found a mother in the Lord in First Lady Olivia Foreman. The church brought an excitement to us and caused us to hope and expect great things as we watched this generational church praise and magnify the Lord from the very youngest child to the oldest adult. We participated in much worship with them over the years and have been encouraged by their demonstration of true fellowship and service to the Lord.

As I pastor Ambassadors of Life in Christ Church, my aspiration is to produce the type of people who understand how they are also connected to the body of Christ. We are never alone in this venture. Thank God for the many men and women of God who stand in rank and file as a spiritual army ready to aid and assist the saints of God. These pages would not be long enough to hold the names of those who have served the Lord so diligently. Yes, there is a great call. It is no doubt that I believe one of these great calls of Jubilee is the call of unity. I do not claim to know more about unity than anyone else. However, I am willing to take the challenge and speak what the Lord has impressed upon my heart after many years of intercession, transitions in ministry, trials of life, and endeavors to see true unity come to pass in the body of Christ. Here are some of the things God has revealed to me about "unity".

1.   Before we can unite with one another, we must unite with Christ.

"Though one may be overpowered by another, two can withstand him. And a threefold cord is not quickly broken."
(Ecclesiastes 4:12)

Everything must have a center; a core element of which it consists. Our center is Jesus. The scripture teach us that a three fold cord is not quickly broken. We need to come together, but we must abide in Him. There is comfort in knowing that my wife, Jacquelyn, stands with me in church ministry. But the true confidence stems from the fact that I know we are both putting our trust, hope, and faith in the Lord, not just one another.

Therefore our marriage can remain strengthened through all the trials we have endured. We have learned though all the setbacks, upsets, and set ups that God is still God and we need not worry about anything because He watches over us in all things.

Well, the church is no different. When we realize God's plan for the church, we can stand secure when we face our storms by staying on the ship with Jesus. Many times, people of God, we give up the ship and go overboard, but the Captain, whose name is Jesus, is able to keep the ship on course, no matter what ship it is. When we are in relationship with Jesus, all is well. As we continue in courtship when we worship Him, He will bring us into fellowship with one another. So these three things are important in unity. Relationship, courtship, and fellowship. You must understand that our love for Jesus must grow so that our love for one another grows.

"Abide in Me , and let My words abide in you, and you shall ask what you will in My name, and I will surely give it to you."
(John 15:1)

We must first make Jesus our pursuit before we pursue unity with one another. Our desire in unity is to let Christ be the center and focus as we walk together in the Lord. If we have Jesus we will lack nothing among ourselves. We have all that we will need as we strive to join together in His plan for each of our lives.

Jesus dealt a lot with unity in John, chapter 17. Jesus thought unity was very important, especially the unity between Him, the Father, and the Holy Spirit. When we understand that God is a God of unity, then we can perceive how to walk in unity with one another. Jesus said, *"I do not pray for these alone, but for those who will believe in Me through their word, that they all may be one, as You, Father, are in Me, and I in You; that they also may be one in Us, that the world may believe that You sent Me."* (John 17:20-21)

So we see that Jesus is one with the Father. He also said, *"He, who is the Spirit of truth... will testify of Me"* (John 15:26). Jesus also unites with the Holy Spirit, and the Holy Spirit only testifies about Christ. Father, Son, Holy Spirit-perfect unity!

Jubilee is the gathering of all of God's people to come together without the restraint of human effort, but through the spiritual obedience to God's Word. A lukewarm church can never be a church of unity. That's why Joel chapter 2 reminds us it must be a church set afire by the Holy Ghost. The Word must become like fire shut up inside our bones, yes, even a living word, burning to the joints and marrows of our bones! God's Word abiding in us will make us united in Christ first before we unite with one another.

2. Holiness always precedes unity because God is not interested in bringing an unclean, unholy church together as one body.

There is a great desire in the body of Christ to see unity. Fellowship with God will always produce a change in a person's life, because when we are truly in the presence of God there is always a spiritual transaction taking place. Holiness is a result of fellowship with God.

In Old Testament times the people of Israel were divided into tribes. Each tribe was divided into families. These divisions did not represent disharmony nor disunity. Each tribe was set aside for particular duties. These divisions assured the responsibility that each tribe and family carried out the mission the Lord God assigned them. It is much like assembling an automobile in the natural. Each specific part must be a whole part, free from all defects and in full working order. They were each separated for God's use. That is what holiness is like. It is like fitting together in God's plan the way He intends for us to fit together.

"In order to unite, we must be a whole unit."

Like many in the body of Christ, I also want to see unity. However, I have now matured enough to realize that the Father God has much work to do on His children before a true sense of unity exists in our local, as well as missionary churches. No matter how much we desire it, we must be honest enough to admit that the church is broken down into fragmented parts, much like a broken vessel. Broken lives; broken dreams; broken hearts. The Lord may join us in our brokenness, but He can not leave us there. There is a healing that needs to take place. He must make the vessel whole again so that it can hold together as He pours His will and destiny into it. The church has an emptiness that only God can fill; a purpose that only God can fulfill. The potter is still molding the church into a unified body that will be able to fit together in unity.

Holiness is wholeness. Holiness is not a denomination, it is a life style. It comes from the Greek word, *"hagiasmos "* which also means sanctification. It is characterized by *"the state predetermined by God for believers, into which grace He calls them, and in which they begin their Christian course and so pursue it. " (Vines Expository dictionary, page 225).*

We are to be separated for God's use. We need to find a place of worship to serve the Lord as He intends for us to do. If you are not attending church, I pray that you might return your heart to the Lord and find one so that you can gladly offer yourself to make a difference in the lives of others. I believe He will lead you in the right direction. He has a plan for your life. Your desire should be to live to please your Father.

In order to understand the significance of this we need to look in this perspective: we are a chosen priesthood, a people of royalty in Jesus. In order to be a priest, you must follow certain criteria. I am not speaking in regard to the Old Testament only, but again in its foreshadowing of New Testament revelation. We are all priests to God, therefore those who lead us have come out from us. We will make excuses because we are not the preacher! We will judge the preacher, but we will not judge ourselves. God sees us all the same. As with the people, so with the prophet, and as with the prophet, so with the priests. It does not matter who you are. We all face the same trials and temptations. But we must all look to ourselves and find our place in Him. It is a holy place. God's desire for each entity of the body of Christ is to perfect holiness in our lives (2 Corinthians 7:1). Holiness is not an impossible task, not even for our children. I am not saying they will *never fall*, but we can show them how to *never fail*!

*"My little children, do not sin! But **if anyone sins**, he has an advocate (lawyer) with the Father, which is Jesus Christ, the Righteous One."* (1 John 2:1-2)

The word of God is clear. God will only bring us together when we are willing to live our lives for Him and receive His word as a catalyst for change. When God speaks the message of salvation, the invitation is for everyone. However we must be reminded that the invitation is an invitation for change.

3. The body of Christ must hear God's voice to be led of the Spirit of God.

The herald trumpet is blowing for us to gather as one family, children of the King, to represent Christ Jesus upon the earth. In ancient times, the herald for which this particular trumpet is named was an officer who carried messages and made announcements for important people such as a King. Furthermore, the herald is figuratively one that goes before or is sent before and shows something more is coming, *a forerunner*. As a verb, *herald* means to go before and announce the coming of. Heraldry determines a person's rights to use a certain coat of arms. The Bible tells us to arm ourselves likewise by putting on the Lord Jesus, and making no provision for the flesh. We are ambassadors of reconciliation for Jesus Christ (2 Corinthians 5:17-21) bringing forth a message of redemptive love and divine destiny into the hopeless, often misdirected lives of people everywhere.

The Lord utters His voice before His army. We, the church, have been called to represent Christ, not our fleshly selves. No matter how we slice cake we all came from the same dough. Unity takes recognition that we may not all be the same in our part, but we are all part of the same whole. The word of God was written for our learning. It is not to thrust our own indoctrination upon others, but to bring a revelation of God's intention already established in the content and context of the Holy Scriptures. It is not to bring separation between cultures, ethnicity, and races of people, but to produce truth among all saints of God. It is not to divide the rich from the poor, but to give us all the inheritance we each have in Jesus Christ. It is not to classify the church into great and small; significant and insignificant; needed and unneeded; but to complete the God intended purpose He desires for your life as your Heavenly Father. I always tell the church, "Don't let anyone tell you that you are not important."

"And be found in Him, not having my own righteousness, which is from the law, but that which is through faith in Christ, the righteousness which is from God by faith." (Philippians 3:9)

4. True reconciliation is a result of unity, and unity is a result of the "agape" kind of love.

We are often hearing people talking about reconciliation now, especially among the races. I believe one of the problems we find is that many of our views of reconciliation are tainted by concepts that do not define true reconciliation in Christ. True reconciliation is not cultural, ethnic, racial, nor social. True reconciliation is a spiritual act that ultimately will display itself in natural terms. We cannot bring reconciliation on our own. The roots go deeper than that. It is a redemptive work on the issues of the heart. We certainly will not have time to deal totally with this subject in this book, but hopefully what we share will help us to begin to pursue relationships based on the truth of God's Word. Hopefully, the

Lord will help us to resolve many of the unsettled issues among our own church leaders and lay people who, some genuinely, and some superficially; seek reconciliation in the church and in our world.

We cannot have unity just because we come together. There is a tough kind of love that carries people through tough times, and the only way to know if it is that kind of love is to go through the tough times together. Love is a life-giving force in the midst of difficult circumstances. It is an impossibility to formulate unity when love is missing. We will all face times where it seems impossible to beat the odds against us. No matter what has happened, we will need the love of someone to carry us through. It helps to hold us together in all types of weather. Rain, sleet, snow, hail, tornadoes, earthquakes, droughts, and famines; that's how circumstances come! This also describes the many emotional changes that are catastrophic in their nature. You may become overwhelmed at times, but do not let the times overcome you

Even our youth are oftentimes confronted with the same feelings we have in the midst of the seasons of their lives. They need a strong sense of guidance, direction, and discipleship. They need a strong type of love that will not sway with all of the winds that may blow. Agape love is a tough type of love that blends with all the factors that come against it. It stands resilient to the storms of life. Love is the "bonding glue" that holds us together in unity. Nothing defines our love more than troubles; nothing shapes our love more than trials.

If our love is only one of convenience and of selfish gain, eventually something will happen to try us in the body of Christ and even in our world. Love is never easy, but love is always strong.

That's how I see the love I share with my wife after twenty six years of marriage. Only the "agape" love of God will last through all the adversities of life, and arise from every storm strengthened.

5. True unity requires a genuine commitment!.

Jesus said in John 4:34, *"My food is to do the will of Him who sent Me, and to finish His work."*

Jesus has called all of us to do one work, and that is the work of reconciliation (2 Corinthians 5:18). We ought to show the same type of commitment Jesus did in His earthly ministry in redeeming us from sin. That is the work of reconciliation! Unity will not work if we are not working, and I am not talking about mere workings of the flesh. I find it very difficult to work with people who have no interest in the kingdom of God! It is important that we are all looking for a city whose builder and maker is God. It is God's work, not our own.

We cannot sit on the seat of our do-nothingness and expect God to do His all-ness!
When people are uninterested in investing their time in something, it shows they have a lack of interest. We give our lives to everything, but we are always worn out when it comes to the things of God! Ephesians 4:3 admonishes us in this manner:

"Endeavoring to keep the unity of the Spirit in the bond of peace."

The word "endeavor" means to work hard toward something. We give up so easily when we are confronted with the true endeavor of unity. We need not only talk it, we need to also walk it! We are in unity with many because it is a matter of convenience, but the Lord sent people around you before you came in unity with those around you now that were not so convenient for you to be together with in unity. Yes, many of us get worn out when it comes to true unity! We have unity via convenience!

They are convenient because many of them put us in what we call the "limelight". We want to be seen! We want to be noticed, but we don't want to be the church! We no longer want the inconveniences that go along with the Christian way of life. We will make all types of sacrifices for the commodities of our ministries, but if we feel we will gain nothing, we quickly become the "invisible man". Can't find us anywhere! All you get is an answering machine! When you finally do hear from us, all you have is criticism for a time that we haven't even been around- no commitment!

We are so guilty in our churches, in our fellowships, and our conferences for this! Do you really think this following slogan actually came from God? *"I'm not hanging around anyone who isn't going anywhere!"* If you do, think about what I am about to say! I know pastors and spiritual leaders are now using this slogan! Before Jesus came into your life you were not going anywhere either, especially not heaven. If it were not for the grace of God, we would all be headed straight to hell! But Jesus gave us extended time! Jesus, through His loving-kindness, drew you out of many waters, redeemed you from sin, and gave you a right to the tree of life. Pride will cause us to say things like this in the body of Christ.

In fact we will hang around people we know are engrossed in sin because we think they are going somewhere, and it is more convenient for our ministry to be around them. Unity is more than bringing a group of people together; it is the divine working of God's mighty power in His church to establish a people committed to the ministry of Jesus Christ.

Jesus is committed to His people . We are still learning how to be committed to one another.

He was gracious enough to forgive us and allow us to work out our problems in the time we have left. You and I may not have done everything right, and we have all offended someone in our lifetime, at least I know I have. But I have repented and went on with my life. That is what salvation is all about. You and I have also been offended in our lives. At least I have. Yes, it hurts, but somehow through the pain I did learn to forgive and release that person to fulfill God's purpose in life. I did not hold them totally responsible for my pain , and I did manage to allow God to show me how to sever the tie that would cause me to think that person owes me something for the offense. I left it totally to the Lord to handle the situation. I leave it up to God to complete His work. I may not always be happy the way He handles it, but I still leave it up to Him. You may not always feel that people are deserving of the blessings God bestows upon them, nor are they deserving of your love because you " remember when". You must allow God to work all of these things out for His purpose and stand back until they are really worked out. God does not need my intervention nor does He need yours. We need His divine intervention in our lives. Unity will require this type of intervention if we are truly committed to seeing unity come to pass in the local church, as well as the outreaches from the local church.

CHAPTER 8

THE TRUMPET CALL OF LIBERTY

"FOR WHERE THE SPIRIT OF THE LORD IS, THERE IS LIBERTY."
(2 CORINTHIANS 3:17)

J ubilee is about restoring liberty. What is liberty? Liberty is the result of not only setting someone free, but giving them the rights and privileges equal to one's self. Aren't you ready to be set free and see others set free? That's what Jesus did. He gave us **a right to the tree of life** because He overcame death, and He is the resurrection and the life. Man fell through Adam, but through Jesus we have been given **the right to become the children of God.** If we don't know our God-given rights, we will continue to suffer outside of our liberty. The trumpet of Jubilee is resounding the voice of liberty to every man, woman, boy, and girl in our generation.

1. Our liberty is always in jeopardy because of "satanic influence".

Bondage is the great enemy to liberty in the Holy Spirit. When bondage creeps into our lives, it slowly causes decay to set into our relationship with the Lord. That is why it is such a useful weapon to Satan. Once Satan has found a place of entry into our lives, he meticulously digs a hole into our minds, and there he sets up camp to destroy us by infiltrating our thought life. Once he finds a workable scheme, he overrides our ability to hear from God. Notice I did not say he overrides our ability to think for ourselves. Man is a "think tank". He will think for himself. But Satan uses this mechanism called 'thought' to captivate our attention through spiritual data input called "satanic influence".

Influence is better than control to Satan because now he can cause one to believe the thought is their own. The Bible tells us that, as sinners, we were held captive by the devil's will and not our own will. You may believe that you are doing what you want to do, but you are simply following the instructions of an infiltrator, namely Satan. How do I break free from this illegal entry into my thought life? Satan is trespassing, whether you believe he conducts his affairs from afar away, or he sends demons or "angels of light " to accomplish his scheme. The Bible declares victory over satanic influence:

"For the weapons of our warfare are not carnal, but they are mighty through God, to the pulling down of strongholds, casting down vain imaginations, and every high thought that exalts itself against the knowledge of God, bringing every thought into captivity to the obedience of Christ." (2 Corinthians 10: 4-5)

Racism, prejudice, bigotry, social injustice, impure and defiled lifestyles to name a few all hinder us in living our lives totally for Jesus Christ.

The scriptures themselves give us a clear understanding of schemes of wickedness that we need to be watchful in Galatians 5:19, 20:

"Now the works of the flesh are evident, which are adultery, for-nication, uncleanness, lewdness, idolatry, sorcery, hatred, con-tentions, jealousies, outbursts of wrath, selfish ambitions, dissen-sions, heresies, envy, murders, drunkenness, revelries, and the like; of which I tell you beforehand, just as I told you in time past, that those who practice such things will not inherit the kingdom of God."

You must take authority in the Name of Jesus and cast down de-monic influences that come against you. The Scripture declares, "Draw near to God and He will draw near to you. Resist the devil and he will flee." Once you have been freed from these negative thoughts, you need to run! Run as fast as you can, and get as close as you can to Jesus! Yes, leave a blazing trail, because now that you are free, Satan will try everything to get you back! Get close to the Lord! The knowledge of the Lord frees me from the hand of the devil! That is what the devil was trying to stop you from doing, knowing the Lord! And once you are close, stay close! The devil is walking about as a roaring lion seeking whom he may de-vour (1 Peter 5:6-14). Those who resist steadfast in the faith! Don't resist the faith, resist the devil. Stop fighting what God is trying to teach you. It will protect you from the enemy!

2.   Liberty is the ability to operate in the sphere of God's rights to the fullest measure with the most com-plete result.

If you are still struggling to reach your purpose, and to realize your destiny, though you may be free, you do not have liberty. Over the years one of my most consistent words to my sons, James and Reginald has been, "With freedom comes responsibility." This is what we must also see about liberty. It is "freedom with responsibility." We have rights, but we must protect those rights by being responsible for our actions. Also in order to gain the right to become sons and daughters of God, we must give up our own rights! Whose rights are you following- your rights or God's rights? Romans 8:1 says, *"There is therefore no condemnation to them that walk not after the flesh, but after the Spirit."* In the preamble of our constitution it states that "...there are, inherent to man, certain inalienable rights, endowed by our Creator; life, liberty, and the pursuit of happiness..."

Many of us have used this to pursue our own freedom of self-indulgence, without responsible living! God wants you and me to live a life of responsibility. People will attempt to place you behind walls for life to take your freedom, however, in responsibility you can take charge of your life again through the liberating power of God in Jesus Christ! With the apostolic call upon the early church, came a greater responsibility to ensure that the Spiritual enactment of the work of Jesus Christ was embedded in the liberty of operating under the sovereign power of the Holy Spirit poured upon the church on the day of Pentecost in Acts 2. This is so evident by the repetition of Joel 2: 28 (NKJV):

"And it shall come to pass afterward that I will pour out My Spirit upon all flesh; your sons and your daughters shall prophesy, your old men shall dream dreams, your young men shall see visions, and also on My menservants and on My maidservants I will pour out My Spirit in those days."

3. In reality, liberty is total restoration to the whole-ness of a person's livelihood.

Restoration is a process that may take years in a person's life. Just as the builder restores the former beauty of a piece of priceless architecture, so the design of our lives may take time to come into full manifestation of the glory the Lord wants to reveal in us. Restoration, however, will come. You may think at this moment that you will never be whole again, but God can make you whole again! "It may take a miracle", you may say! Well, God special-izes in the impossible, and He would love to make a miracle out of you! All you need to do is act like the woman with the issue of blood. You see, Jesus was not impressed with the crowd, but He was impressed by the one woman! She touched the interlining threads crested upon the ground beneath His priestly robe! It was just one touch! " He will not notice ", she thought, "if I only touch the very edge of His garment!" Oh, what faith she had! But Jesus responded! He first responded without a word spoken! The virtue went out of Him to touch her! That virtue made her com-pletely whole! With all the people around her, Jesus was sensitive to her touch! With all the crowds of people, Jesus was still able to touch one person with the deepest need for wholeness! This is truly restoration!

4. Restoration comes through a process called trans-formation!

We cannot really restore anything broken without first altering its form. Jesus can not really restore us without transforming us. The Father is not going to pour new wine into old wineskins. How-ever, He is not going to destroy the old wineskin either. God works generationally. The former work and the latter work of the spirit of God are both important. The Bible tells us that a wise scribe will bring out of his treasure things both new and old.

Restoration involves a process of change that spans into the life-time of a person. When Jesus Christ redeemed us, He redeemed the whole person- past, present, and future! In other words, you were saved, you are saved, and you are being saved through one single act of atonement or reconciliation. This is one act of recon-ciliation that is three-fold. Jesus redeemed you totally from sin to righteousness, you are now being victorious over sin through righteousness, yet sin has to still be eradicated from your life by righteousness in Christ. You must experience liberty in a total way in your life.

Jesus did a spiritual work of redemption called salvation, which leads to the natural work called sanctification, until it finally re-sults in a supernatural work called transformation.

Transformation happens supernaturally just as it does naturally. First comes the seed, then the root, and afterwards the tree. In the year of Jubilee they ate the produce that grew freely in the land. God wants us to grow and mature supernaturally, without human interference of man's philosophical, and theoretical views being planted in our lives. The Word of God must be engrafted in our hearts so that we can bring forth much fruit to God! Let us get rid of the excuses! We can live for God!

CHAPTER 9

THE PROPHETIC TRUMPET OF BLESSING
"SOWING SEEDS OF DESTINY"

"BEHOLD, HOW BEAUTIFUL AND PLEASANT IT IS FOR
BRETHREN TO DWELL TOGETHER IN UNITY. FOR THERE THE LORD
COMMANDS THE BLESSING, EVEN LIFE FOREVERMORE."
(PSALMS 133:1, 4)

As long as we are held back in our purpose we can never reach our goals in life. The year of Jubilee is demonstrated in <u>the blessings that are released upon the people</u> as they are canceled from debts, their mortgages are released, and their liberty is regained in their homes, and community. Furthermore we should be reminded of God's great destiny He has intended for the church of Jesus Christ. The Bible tells us that we must speak those things that be not as though they were. We must lift our voices and openly declare who Jesus is in our lives. In Revelation, when Satan launches his greatest attack upon the church, it states that they overcame him by the word of their testimony, and by the blood of the Lamb, and they loved not their lives unto death (see Revelation 12:11). Our "*jubilee*" would not be complete without the testimony of God's awesome power in our lives! Remember, the Lord does not only want to give you earthly possessions, but heavenly blessings as well.

The prophetic voice of Father God is blowing today resounding with the bestowment of heavenly blessings as He speaks sovereignly to the purpose of the church. The prophetic voice is speaking to the church to declare faithfully the deeds of the Lord performed in Her midst. Blessings have always been an important part of celebration.

Our proclamation of who we are in Christ Jesus is so foundational in our receiving blessings from God, because the blessings are for the apparent heirs of the kingdom of God.

Paul declared these words in I Corinthians 15:10:

"But by the grace of God I am what I am, and His grace toward me was not in vain; but I labored more abundantly than they all, yet not I, but the grace of God which was with me."

If you are not sure of who you are, then you must declare it with me now:

1. "I am a child of God."

"What gives me the liberty to say I am a child of God?", you may say. I am sure there are some who may not immediately agree with you. Some of those people may be the ones who know you best or think they know you most. There may even be those who believe you are undeserving of God's grace.

However consider Paul's statement. Paul's brand of identity is indeed remarkable and leaves much for us to consider. First of all, Paul did not pass "the eye test." Look at how they judged Paul's bodily appearance. *"For his letters," they say, "are weighty and powerful, but his bodily presence is weak, and his speech is contemptible."* (I Corinthians 10:10) That is often the way others may assess us these days. They may think they know you simply by looking you. How amazing! What powerful people we are indeed! Well, Paul did not consider the eye test to determine if he was a child of God.

Next, look at Paul's history (see Galatians 1:13; Acts 9:1). He persecuted the church of God. He was there when Stephen the Martyr gave his life for preaching the gospel of Jesus Christ. It would seem such a past disqualified him for a son, but it did not. Thank God he does not look at our past to determine our future. I am sure there were those in hs day who wanted to stop him from fulfilling his destiny, who felt he did not deserve God's best.
Aren't you glad that man does not have the final say in your identity with Jesus Christ? The bible says in John 1:12, *"But as many as received Him, to them He gave a right to become children of God, to those who believe in His name."* Praise the Lord forever! I thank Him for that!

Thirdly, Paul accredited his worth to the grace of God, not the opinions of men. Life can be difficult enough when we are striving to do the right things, and the wrong things happen. Good things will happen, but sometimes things do not go according to plan. When you and I realize the grace of God as Paul did, we will not falter in our identity with Christ even in the difficult times. Your faith in Him can remain strong when you rely on His grace. The same grace that obtained salvation is the same grace that will sustain you through your trials. That same grace will cause you to retain the Word of God in your life so that you can maintain your relationship with Jesus. The ultimate aim of the grace of God is that you remain connected to Him who is the source of all you are and ever will be.

So you may know that He died for the sins of the world, but do you acknowledge that He personally died for your sins? Many of the messages we hear teach us that God loves us in spite of our sins, but redemption actually came because of sin, not in spite of sin. God does not love you any more now that you are saved: you just love Him more! You now know the love of God! If you are reading this book, and you do not know the love of God, then you can receive that love right now! Now is *the time of salvation*!

The first destiny you and I must secure is eternal destiny. Everything else is secondary. I must invite you to decide where you will spend eternity, with Jesus in Heaven, or with Satan in the lake of fire where agony never ceases. When you believe with the heart that God raised Jesus from the dead to save you from death, and confess that you receive Him as Lord of your life, a spiritual rebirth has taken place. Then your confession should be, "I am a child of God" (Romans 10:9-11). Pray this prayer with me:

> **"Lord Jesus, I come to you today realizing I am a sinner with all my faults and all my sins I have committed. I come recognizing that you love me with all of my sins, and all my faults. In fact, this is the very reason you died for me, according to John 3:16 KJV (For God so loved the world that He gave His only begotten Son that whosoever believeth on Him should not perish, but they shall have everlasting life). I believe you**

gave your life for my life as a ransom, and now I serve you. I open my heart for you to come in and be my Savior, my Lord, and my friend. In Jesus name. Amen."

Your time of Jubilee is here! Rejoice! Jesus has set you free from the oppression of the devil! You are now free to serve the Lord with gladness and thanksgiving in your heart. If you prayed this prayer, please write to us, so that we can under gird you with prayer and help you find a local church. When you connect to the vision of God in a church family and share your testimony of salvation, this will strengthen you in your faith. It is always good knowing you have others standing with you in the kingdom of God.

2. "I am blessed with all spiritual blessings."

Ephesians 1:3 says, *"Blessed be the God and the Father of our Lord Jesus Christ, who has blessed us with every spiritual blessing in heavenly places."* This is so powerful for us as Christians, to realize that our blessings are truly not dependent on worldly standards. In the way of the world, many of us would never experience a time of jubilee, because we would not feel deserving by the views our world impose upon us. In the business world, you must reach a certain quota, or satisfy the expectation of your employer through productivity. Your productivity is measured by the quality and quantity expected. You get what you deserve (at least that is what they tell you) by whatever the standard of reward. In order to get rewarded, all you have to do is what is expected of you. You might not get the reward you deserve. Many of us who are blue collar or white collar workers, if we are truly honest with ourselves know that, after years of services for organizations, institutions, and corporations, we are still not being paid what we are worth! Not only are you not getting blessed, you are losing your reward! In describing this system of economics the rich are getting richer and the poor are getting poorer. Our lower and middle class echelon of our society is always where the most growth takes place. Profit sharing and buying stocks is supposed to make you feel you are getting a piece of the "economic pie", and you are truly a part of the investment plan of the company. These are often practical and wise ways of investment, but often the risks are unknowns, and even a venture of this magnitude requires spiritual fortitude in the time in which we live. We also must not become consumed in risky private investments and "get-rich-quick" schemes! God does not really desire that the people of God be held totally in bondage to this world system. Money must remain a commodity to the church; it must not become a god!

It's time we realize that there is a great difference between earthly rewards and blessings.

The Bible tells us that *"The blessings of the Lord makes rich, and adds no sorrow with it."* (Proverbs 10:22).

Here's something to think about:

- *Sometimes getting a reward can be like inheriting someone else's headache.*

- *However a blessing is much more than what you deserve.*
- *As a matter of fact, if some of us got what we deserved, we would be in big trouble!*

- *A reward is for anyone, but a blessing is for the faithful.*

Some of us want ours right now always, and that is why we end up with only our reward. But many saints of God, have served the Lord faithfully in fellowship in the church, bringing tithes and offerings, living lives exceptionally in Christ through times of testing. While still maintaining a desire to perfect holiness and pursue a closer walk with Christ, they have been tested in their attitude, character, and trust in Him. They have suffered faithfully with all types of mistreatment and unfairness in their personal relationships, in their communities, on their jobs, and some even in the church. Does that sound like you? Never mind the fact that you are not always perfect. Do you truly love the Lord? Is your life one that strives to be as Christ desires you to be? Are you still placing your trust in Him?

These are the specific people the Lord is declaring He will bless in the time of jubilee. It really matters who we trust, doesn't it?

"Some trust in chariots (the influence and persuasion of someone in a higher position of power or authority), and some in horses (their own strength to produce results), but we trust in the name of the Lord our God!" (Psalm 20:7)

People may be able to hinder you from getting your earthly reward, but they can never touch your blessing! That belongs to you! Like the song says, "What God has for me, it is for me", whether you think I deserve it or not! The only reward greater than the blessings of God are the Heavenly rewards you receive in eternity, so please don't lose your crown!

3. "I am not limited, but I am fulfilled in Jesus Christ."

Jubilee sets us free from the restraints others have placed upon us. "You will never make it!" "It can't be done!" "That's too much for you!" Discouragement is a great enemy to success. You can do all things through Christ who will give you the strength. Overcoming obstacles is difficult for the weary mind. I'm sure that Joshua felt this way when the mantle of Moses was placed upon him to bring the people of God into the promised land. The responsibility was too great! However we all realize that nothing can naturally prepare us for the ultimatum The Lord places on our lives to obey and follow Him, just as no one can truly train you to care for a child not yet born. They may instruct you, but much of it stays on the shelf until the time appointed by the Father. So it is with our Spiritual lives. Jubilee is an appointed time in our lives. Nothing can aid you in overcoming all of your insufficiencies except a working relationship with Christ in which He is obligating Himself to equip you for every impossibility that comes your way. As He said to Joshua , *"Be strong, and be very courageous, for the Lord your God is with you wherever you go." (Joshua 1:9b)*

4. "I am a steward of God's Word, therefore success will follow me."

God's promise to Joshua is that He would give Him the land! Stewardship is part ownership, however you look at it! God does not give His children half of a blessing! My stewardship in Christ is not like the system of man, because man will ask you to take care of something for him, and leave you with no inheritance in the end. That is why the year of Jubilee is so important! This is God's way of saying, "I take care of those who are faithful to

Me!" If you have been faithful to God, you should know He will provide for you in all things. God will not commit anything to your trust without committing Himself to your trust. Man will, but God won't! God committed the people of Israel to Joshua's care, but not without a promise:

"Be strong and of good courage, for to this people you shall divide as an inheritance the land which I swore to their fathers to give them. Only be strong and very courageous, that you may observe to do according to all the law which Moses My servant commanded you; do not turn from the right hand or to the left, that you may prosper wherever you go. This book of the law shall not depart from your mouth, but you shall meditate in it day and night, that you may observe to do all that is written in it. For then you shall make your way prosperous, and then you will have good success." (Joshua 1:6-8)

Make God's Word a daily part of your life. Read it! Study it! Meditate upon it! It will cause you to be successful in all that you do.

5. "I am a part of a holy nation to bring honor, glory, and praise to God my Father."

Where do you stand on the scales of humanity? How do others view you in the total picture of life-as a shadow, maybe as a mere background, or simply something abstract without any particular meaning? This declaration is a confirmation of your position relative to the nations. No matter the shadows of your past, or the family background from which you came, or the confusing state of affairs that may have brought you here, you are divinely significant to God. In view of all of the nations of the world, the greatest nation is THE NATION OF SALVATION. Redemption sets you in a holy position apart from the political, social, and even cultural pressures of that natural nation where you live. 1 Peter 2:9 says, "But you are a chosen generation, a royal priesthood, a holy nation, His own special people, that you may proclaim the praises of Him who called you out of darkness into His marvelous light." Though in essence you are not above the law of the land, the orchestration of your life is beyond the boundaries of life in which you are naturally accustomed.

6. "I am filled with the life of God through the Holy Spirit in me."

Where the Spirit of the Lord is, there is liberty. The Holy Spirit is doing something awesome in the body of Christ today. It is unusual, yet still very welcoming to see. He is getting the body of Christ hungry for more than a usual diet! God's people are really beginning to hunger for the truth of God's Word again. This is fertile ground for a spiritual work to be done in the saints that would cause us to mature enough to know what God's ultimate desire truly is for the church A spiritual desire has been created by hungry hearts still not satiated by just the talents, poise, and gifts of God upon man called the anointing.

The true saints are hungering for the very essence of Christ to dwell in and among His people.

There must always be a spiritual exchange happening between me and my Lord. My life for His life! This is something the church has lost and has fought to regain for years. We have gathered in mass numbers in prayers, praise and worship, conferences, seminars, and workshops, as we have hoped Jesus would come in a manifestation of glory and seal our direction for the next "wave" of the Holy Spirit. Many times we left, though excited and blessed, but still disappointed that we know Jesus no more than when we went "there." We still are not aware of what Jesus is up to! Unfortunately, sometimes the reason is because Jesus didn't start the program, He was just invited! However, sometimes Jesus did start the program, but we forgot to invite Him! And many of us went because we were invited! We got a seat in the sanctuary, but there was no place for Jesus to take His seat in our sanctuary!

There is a place where we come in our lives where no man can take us. You can sing the beauty of the song, but only an open heart will bring you there! Just look at it from the standpoint of a wedding. You may see many people, preachers, and loved ones you think are worthy to participate in your wedding. But in reality, the only two people who will leave that place with a true commitment of love are the bride and groom. That's how it ought to be with every service you attend. When the service is done, you and Jesus will walk together in a renewed commitment to one another, because a spiritual exchange has happened between you. The Holy Spirit has imparted life into you as you open your heart to God with a burning desire to see His will accomplished in your life..

7. "I am complete in Jesus by His anointing at work in my life, therefore I am complete no matter where I go in the world."

Once the Holy Spirit resides, He can begin to work in you. What are the things you feel you will never accomplish in life? Do you worry that not being fulfilled in that area automatically stops God's work in your life? The anointing is still being poured out on you today as it never has before. God is not through with you. Don't limit yourself by the road you are traveling! In Psalm 119:132, David said, " Thy word, O Lord, is a lamp unto my feet, and a light unto my path." There's a whole world out there waiting for you to fill your space, and take your place! As long as God is still at work, there is still hope! What you need now is faith to believe He will move for y-o-u! Jesus is telling you to call those things that be not as though they were. He did not tell you to determine when they will become. Just simply believe!

8. "I am completely free from all things that would hinder me from fulfilling my purpose in life."

If there are indeed difficulties you face in life that seem to hold you in limbo, and take away your progress in what you have set as spiritual goals in your life, please do not give up. Remember that though you are in a stall does not mean you are not in the race! A racing horse is placed in a stall first to get focused on the race. No matter what it is, I will utilize it as a tool of progress! It may not be in line with my purpose right now, and I may even feel I have wasted a great deal of my time. "But ...". That one word can change the way I see my circumstance! But... "all things work together for the good to them who love God , to them who are the called according to His purpose! (Romans 8:28-b)" But... "no weapon formed against me shall prosper!" (Isaiah 54:17-a) But.... "weeping may endure for a night, *but joy* cometh in the morning (Psalm 30:5-b)!"

CONCLUSION

"LET MY PEOPLE GO!"

Yes, children of God, it's time for Jubilee! As we look deeply into our lives, what do we see? A person planning their *time* with great expectations, dreams, and aspirations, or one sitting meagerly by, letting time slip into the darkness of yesterday? Whatever our answer may be, these two kinds of people have one determining factor which will decide where they will be and what will happen to them. It is called the future. And may I ask an even more intense question? Who holds our future? We may answer quickly, "God does!" In order to know who holds our future, we must know who controls our time. We all know we have occupations, whether they be secular or spiritual in nature. The question is, are you being controlled by this world or does your future truly lie in God? For our future lies in the hands of that person, whether it be God, our liberator, or Satan, our oppressor. It lies in the hands of the one who controls our time!

Jubilee is the time when the Lord takes control over our destiny, and releases us from the inward toil of living our days in the vicious circle that leads us to never-never land. This curse on our time must be broken, and our oppressor, Satan and his demons, must let us go free in the name of Jesus Christ.

The future is a questionable thing in our age. At this time, no one is really sure what lies beyond the year 2000. As I mentioned in the beginning, we are on the threshold of time, even as I write these words, in the third day of a new year, 1999. It is a threshold year! In a sense this is a year of Passover. We are passing from an old century into a new century. So this is a year, even as God told Israel to remember the Passover, God wants us to remember Him! He was saying to Israel, "Remember how I freed you from the oppression of Egypt."

Egypt can allegorically symbolize the world system, because the pharaohs of Egypt controlled most of the world's wealth at the time and enslaved people of all races, cultures, and creeds. Can we find examples of this in our world today? Are there systems in place in our world that empower a small amount of people while keeping others grid locked from achieving their goals and dreams? I believe the answer is yes.

Even in America, we face examples of this everyday. I must say that faith does not blind us to injustice. It just helps us to endure it, especially in the African-American culture. Yes, even today, unfortunately, race remains an issue. It is clear in our justice system with more black males serving harsher sentences than white males. We can see it as DNA evidence clears many innocent men and women who have served prison time for crimes they never committed. It is evident still in corporate America. It is obvious with the way the flooding of New Orleans was handled by our government. And yet our faith keeps us strong. But we are not blind!

Also, America is supposed to be a Christian nation founded upon Christian values of her forefathers. I agree this is indeed the premise upon which it was built. Take a real good look. There are restraints placed upon us in our world because we contradict the values and viewpoints concerning praying in public places in the name of Jesus Christ, sharing our faith openly to unbelievers and non-believers in Christ without the hindrances placed upon us in the marketplace, courts, schools, and our communities. This is the land of the free and the home of the brave. However, we are not all the way free.

But God sent Moses to be a deliverer and tell Pharaoh, "Let my people go!' God delivered them by *passing over* the first-born of Israel, when the angel of death saw the blood. This is also a spiritual type of the church of Jesus Christ. Yes, we are living in the midst of a troubled world, but because of the blood of Jesus, we have full coverage. We have full victory. Our Passover lamb has already been sacrificed and His name is Jesus.

Thank God for His loving kindness and tender mercies. God has commissioned us to boldly speak the Word of Jesus Christ in our age. God wants to give us liberty to serve Him without restraint, expressing the joy of the Lord! Our war is waged through the cross of Jesus Christ. God has rolled back the curtains of our disparity and created an open door that leads us into a new kind of world. This is a world where His peace and His purpose is initiated in the midst of a world that does not know nor understand His ways.

I am sure that September 11, 2001 is a day we will remember. My concern is, *"Will we remember the Lord?"* We need to acknowledge God in our schools, in our courts, and in our communities.

Jubilee is a year of remembrance in which we must have recognition, reflection, and revelation. *This is no time for the church to fall asleep!* This is a time when Jesus is doing a work of re-establishment, rebirth, and reconstruction. Jesus is working a work in our day until His day comes, that is, the day of the Lord. No one knows the day nor the hour the Son of Man will appear. Jesus is on the Father's apostolic time clock, and we are on the prophetic time clock of Jesus Christ. The sounding of the trumpet is a signature of the end-times. After the seven seals, there will be seven trumpets that will proclaim judgment on the world in Revelation chapter 8 to 11. But the finest hour of the church is when she sits as the bride of Christ at the marriage supper of the Lamb (Revelation 19:7). This is the pinnacle of our desire to become one with the Lamb of God as we complete the wedding ceremony in one glorious feast. Here every nation will have a representative, every person will have a voice and every life will be significant! I tell you, this will be worth waiting for! This will be worth all of the pain and sacrifice! Yes, the glory of being in the presence of the King of King and the Lord of Lords will be worth it all!

In 1 Corinthians 15: 51-53, it declares, "Behold, I tell you a mystery: we shall not all sleep, but we shall all be changed - in a moment, in the twinkling of an eye, at the last trumpet. For the trumpet will sound, and the dead will be raised incorruptible, and we shall all be changed." In fact, we are being changed this very moment by the quickening of the Holy Spirit. He is the life-giving power in us.

The very purpose of Jubilee is to cause us to experience divine change in our lives that brings the liberty of the Holy Spirit to life in us! It is to be jubilant; full of expression! It is to be full of joy! The Lord wants our worship to be so magnificent that none of the pressures of life can dissipate the glory of God in our lives!

As the day of the Lord approaches we ought to give the more earnest heed to sound doctrine! Our time is short. Jesus is soon to return. He is calling for His children to be mature enough to be a bride. He is not looking for the same child He saved from sin. He is looking for a bride that has made herself ready with the glory of the Lord. That is who Jesus is looking for in the church. He is not looking for a whining baby. He is looking for, as Lady Olivia Foreman, my spiritual mother in the Lord would say, "a bride in combat boots!"

So what should we be doing? How shall we celebrate? We should be attentive to what the Spirit of the Lord is saying to the church. Get beyond the ascetics and the crowds of people and understand that this is the time of rejoicing in our lives, a time to draw closer in knowing the Lord. It is time, not for personal freedom, but for responsible living in the liberty of the Holy Spirit. You may have struggled to this point, but you are at the threshold of your blessing. Don't turn back now! Stand firm! God has a call upon your life, even if it is just to be a vessel of the Holy Spirit to release the presence of the Lord where you are. Let us make the vessel ready by filling it with fresh oil. For the Lord has given you the oil of gladness to replace the spirit of sorrow. It is a time for you to put on the garment of praise, and celebrate the victories of your life over oppression, no matter how difficult it may seem to you. Step out on faith and move into this field of fruitfulness in your life. God will not only reward you. He will also load you with His blessings that are waiting for you. Children of God, it is time for Jubilee!

.

Cyril R. Howell, Sr. is the sixth child of ten children of his parents, late Paul and Betty Howell, and a native of Shelby, North Carolina. He is married to Jacquelyn Scott Howell where they reside in McLeansville, NC. He is the father of four adult children; James, Reginald, Precious, and Princess and the grandfather of four wonderful grandchildren; Jaquan, Terrell, Janaya and Antonio.

Although he grew up in the church all of his life, it was while on the campus of North Carolina A & T State University, November 1979, when he received Jesus Christ as his personal savior. It was also upon this very campus, in 1980, that he was baptized in the Holy Spirit and received the call of God to preach and teach the Word of God.

He has served in the local church community as leader of intercessory prayer, lay minister, deacon, usher, ordained elder, and assistant pastor. Cyril is ordained in the office of Prophet and the pastor of Ambassadors of Life in Christ Church in Greensboro, North Carolina.

He holds a degree in Professional Biology as well as Teaching Biology; 16 years of experience in lab technology and is currently 8years certified teacher and teaching Biology in the Guilford County Schools in Greensboro, North Carolina.

Cyril is a sought after speaker at churches, conferences, and seminars. His message brings purpose, direction, healing, and deliverance to the body of Christ. He believes we are in the season of the end-time harvest and God is still saving the souls of men and women all over the world. He endeavors to live his life as an example of Jesus Christ and to please Him by fulfilling the great commission of reconciliation unto God.

BIBLIOGRAPHY

Thomas Nelson Quick Reference Edition New King James, The Holy Bible, Copyright@2000 by Thomas Nelson, Inc.

The New Strong's Exhaustive Concordance of the Bible, by James Strong, LL.D., S.T.D., Copyright@1990 by Thomas Nelson Publishers, Nashville, Camden, Kansas City

Vines Expository Dictionary of Old and New Testament Words by W. E. Vine, Old Testament edited by F. F. Bruce, Copyright@1981 by Fleming H. Revell Company, Old Tappan, New Jersey

www.ingramcontent.com/pod-product-compliance
Lightning Source LLC
Chambersburg PA
CBHW032013040426
42448CB00006B/621